Murder & Crime
LANCASHIRE

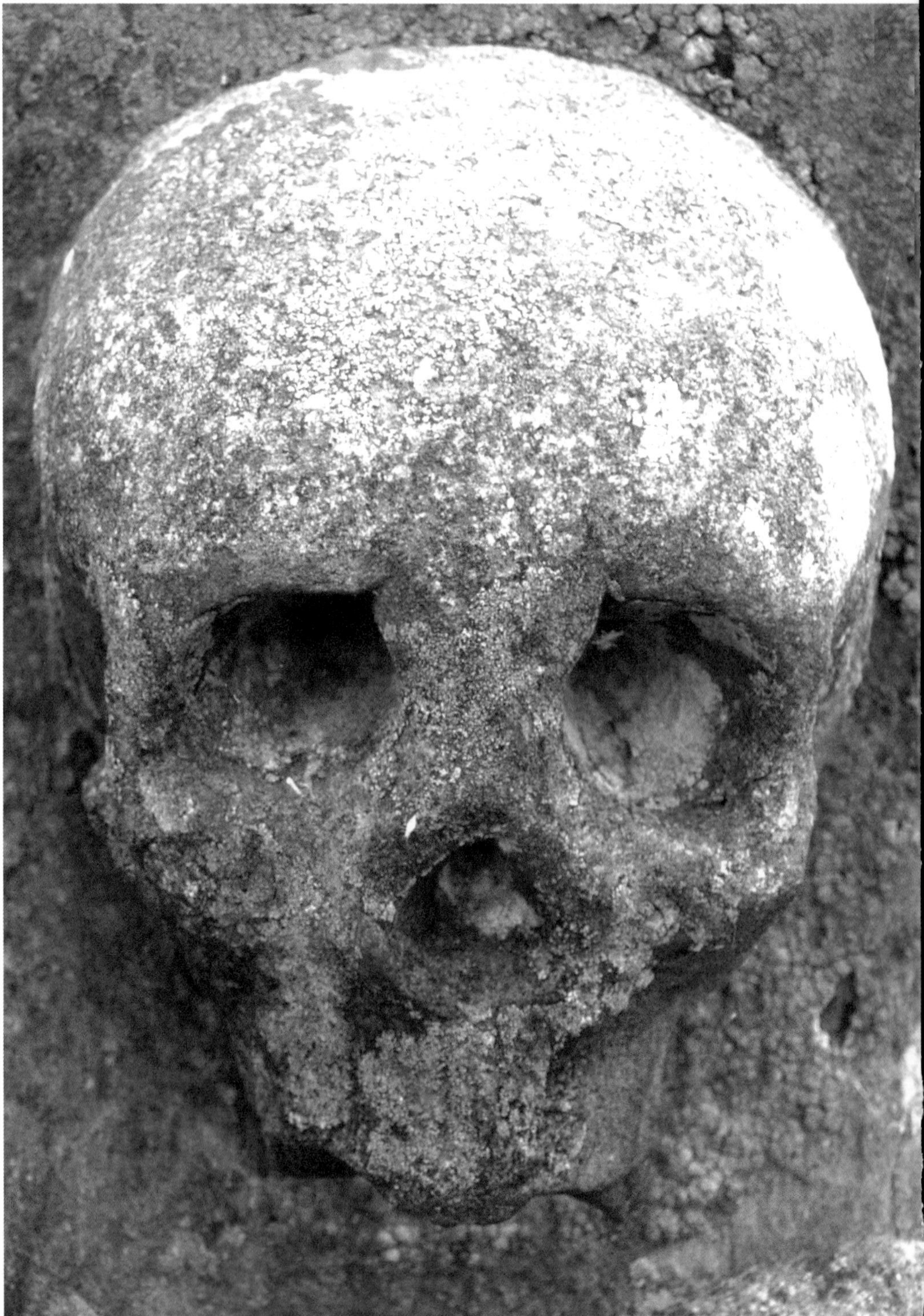

Murder & Crime
LANCASHIRE

MARTIN BAGGOLEY

TEMPUS

This is for Peter, Al, Jim, Margaret, Joan and Mike, all friends from the Lancashire of my youth.

Frontispiece: Photograph by kind permission of Victoria Amador.

First published 2007

Tempus Publishing
Cirencester Road, Chalford,
Stroud, Gloucestershire, GL6 8PE
www.tempus-publishing.com

Tempus Publishing is an imprint of NPI Media Group

© Martin Baggoley, 2007

The right of Martin Baggoley to be identified as the Author of this work has been asserted in accordance with the Copyrights, Designs and Patents Act 1988.

All rights reserved. No part of this book may be reprinted or reproduced or utilised in any form or by any electronic, mechanical or other means, now known or hereafter invented, including photocopying and recording, or in any information storage or retrieval system, without the permission in writing from the Publishers.

British Library Cataloguing in Publication Data.
A catalogue record for this book is available from the British Library.

ISBN 978 0 7524 4358 4

Typesetting and origination by NPI Media Group
Printed in Great Britain

CONTENTS

one	Murder at The Jolly Carter, Winton, 1826	7
two	The Harpurhey Mystery, 1880	19
three	The Sweethearts' Deadly Tiff, Southport, 1886	35
four	Mass Murder and Suicide in Salford, 1888	43
five	The Ticket of Leave Man, Bolton, 1890	53
six	The Dark Hole Clough Horror, Manchester, 1893	63
seven	A Double Hanging in Liverpool, 1904	71
eight	The Yorkshire Street Robbery, Oldham, 1913	77
nine	'Little Annie is Missing', Darwen, 1932	87
	Bibliography	95

ACKNOWLEDGEMENTS

I am grateful to the staff of the British Newspaper Library, Colindale, for their assistance, and the Local Studies Libraries of Manchester, Oldham and Rochdale for permission to use their photographs. Thanks also to Geoff Parker for his help with the illustrations. I am also indebted to my editor, Cate Ludlow.

I

MURDER AT THE JOLLY CARTER, WINTON, 1826

The Jolly Carter, an old country inn which had previously been known as the Sun Inn and the Rising Sun, stood 150 yards from the Bridgewater Canal, in the hamlet of Winton, near Eccles. The landlord, Joseph Blears, lived on the premises with his wife Martha, together with two members of staff, thirty-four-year-old Elizabeth Bate and William Higgins, aged fourteen years. It was a respectable and orderly establishment, and the landlord, his wife and their employees were popular and respected throughout the neighbourhood. On 22 May 1826, however, it became the scene of a most horrific murder and an attempted murder, crimes of such brutality that they shocked not only the surrounding district but the whole country.

The inn was used by many local organisations and societies, and it was widely known that Joseph Blears often kept the funds of several of these groups in a strongbox in his bedroom. The Orange Society had held a public dinner on the previous Saturday, at which £25 was raised. Additionally, the funds of a sick club for local women, which met at the inn, and to which members contributed 2s each quarter, had recently been collected, and they were also in the strongbox. On the night of the crime there was thus a large amount of cash on the premises.

That night Joseph was in Manchester on business, and at 7.30 p.m. a stranger walked in and, speaking in a broad Scottish accent, ordered a drink, before sitting at a table on his own. Thirty minutes later he was joined by another man who was well known to staff and customers as Alec and after asking for a drink, he sat at the table with the other man. At the time, there were three other customers in the bar, Thomas Partington, Robert Wilson and Jesse Jones.

It had been one year earlier that Alec first visited the Jolly Carter. He was a hawker who had attempted to persuade Joseph and Martha to buy some of his wares. They were not interested but he offered to exchange a pair of fine stockings with Martha in return for a canary which was kept in a cage on the bar. This was agreed to, and since then he had been a regular visitor to the inn.

After completing his business in Manchester, Joseph took the Worsley packet along the Bridgewater Canal, from which he alighted near to the Jolly Carter at 8 p.m. When he arrived a few minutes later he sent William to bed. 'Alec' was in fact thirty-year-old Alexander McKeand and the stranger was his twenty-four-year-old brother Michael. Alexander engaged Joseph in conversation, and insisted on buying him several glasses of whisky. Thomas Partington noticed the two men pouring some of their own drinks into Joseph's glass, but at the time, believing they

The Jolly Carter in 1826.

Right: Joseph Blears.

Below: Martha Blears.

Opposite below: The Bridgewater Canal, close to the Jolly Carter, where Joseph Blears stepped off the packet from Manchester on the night of the murder. The building to the left, which is visible through the railings, is a pub which was built in the 1850s, and which was named the Packet House in recognition of the location's importance in the area.

William Higgins.

were simply being generous, did not find this suspicious. Within a relatively short time, however, Joseph was drunk and fell into a deep sleep in the bar.

At 11 p.m. Partington, Wilson and Jones left. A few minutes later, the McKeands asked Martha if they could sleep at the Jolly Carter, as they did not wish to return to Manchester, for it was by now dark. They agreed to sleep in the same room as young William, and Betty was asked to take them upstairs. She believed that both men were following her, but although Alexander did so, Michael remained downstairs, and hid himself from Martha, who was in the bar together with her still sleeping husband.

Upstairs, Betty walked into the bedroom and was immediately attacked by Alexander. As there was a lighted candle in the room and William was awake, he was able to provide a graphic description of what occurred. When the youngster first saw the couple struggling, he presumed that the visitor was trying to force his attentions on Betty. He heard her saying, 'Give over and be quiet'. He could see that Alexander had his left arm around her throat, and a few moments later his right hand moved towards her neck. At first William did not see the knife in Alexander's hand, but within seconds he saw blood gushing from a severe throat wound.

He watched as Alexander threw Betty to the floor, as she screamed, 'Murder, murder'. She continued to fight for her life and grabbed her attacker's legs. As she struggled to pull herself up she screamed, 'I'll mark thee, man'. He threw her to the floor again, and stabbed her once more in the throat.

Thinking she was dead, Alexander left Betty and moved towards a petrified William, who was frozen in terror in his bed. Alexander held him down, covering the boy's mouth with his left hand – in the other hand he held the knife. William's life was only saved by the fact that Betty was not quite dead: struggling to her feet, she staggered out of the bedroom and made towards another

Monton Bridge.

upstairs room. Alexander had to leave William before he could hurt him further, and ran over to Betty to finish her off. William, now free to move, took the opportunity to run for his life.

The lad pushed past the struggling man and woman, and managed to evade Alexander's attempt to grab him by his nightshirt, but who in so doing, left a bloody imprint of his hand on it. William jumped over the banister and ran down the stairs. On reaching the ground floor, he rushed through the kitchen and out of the back door. He ran to a nearby field in which he hid, and from where he watched in great fear as Alexander emerged from the inn to look for him. However, when Michael joined him, they decided to make their escape and fled into the darkness.

Inside the inn, Martha had been alerted by Betty's screams and had picked up a lighted candle. She had run towards the stairs, but before she could reach them, Michael grabbed hold of her. He pushed her to her knees, and stabbed her in the neck. He withdrew the knife and stabbed her again, this time in the forehead. Next, he stabbed her in the face, just under her eye, and when he attempted to pull the knife out, the handle broke off. Despite his determined efforts, he was unable to withdraw it from his victim and ran from the scene, leaving the blade embedded in the unfortunate woman's face.

Martha ran outside to raise the alarm, where she was joined by William. They called at the house of her neighbour and niece, Mary Andrews, and the local constable, William Brittain, was summoned. On his arrival, the four of them entered the building, and at this time, the knife was still protruding from Martha's face.

Upstairs they found Betty's body in a large pool of blood, and nearby was a black leather stock. Downstairs, they found a yellow stick. Later William Hancock, who had shared rooms with the McKeands in Salford, would identify both of these items as having belonged to Alexander. The following morning, in a field at the rear of the inn, a distinctive black handkerchief was discovered, and William Hancock identified this as having belonged to Michael. Also in the field, searchers found the footprints of the two men, which they were able to follow as far as Monton Bridge, about one mile away, indicating they had travelled north, and were probably making for their native Dumfries.

In view of the seriousness of the crimes, Manchester's Deputy Constable Stephen Lavender was put in charge of the investigation. He went to the McKeands' lodgings in Salford, but not surprisingly they could not be found. However, he received a tip from one of their neighbours, which led him to the house of Sarah Stewart, wife of local cutler, James Stewart. The knife was a vital piece of evidence, and Mrs Stewart provided invaluable information about it. She had known Michael McKeand for several years, and she confirmed that on the Saturday before the murder, she had helped her husband at an auction of some of his cutlery. She identified the knife that had been used to wound Martha, and which was obviously new, as being the one that had been stolen at the auction. At the time she had suspected Michael, who had been with her, and who had had the opportunity to take it.

The inquest into Betty's death was held at the Jolly Carter on the Wednesday following the crimes, before the local coroner John Milne. Evidence was given by those who had been in the inn on the night, and this included the identification of the McKeand brothers as the chief suspects. Details of the physical evidence that had been discovered were also provided. It was also at the inquest that details of the horrific nature of the attacks made on both women were disclosed by Dr John Garthside, who had arrived on the scene at shortly after midnight.

He discovered that the knife had been driven into Martha's face with such force that it had penetrated the strongest part of her cheekbone, in a slanting direction, and had lodged in the back of her mouth. That this had prevented her assailant from withdrawing the knife, thus rendering him unable to continue stabbing her, had undoubtedly saved her life. Before the doctor, two other men had tried unsuccessfully to pull the knife out. The doctor also failed to do so, until he decided to grip Martha's head very tightly whilst his assistant pulled it out after a great deal of effort. Once the knife had been taken out, he was able to treat her wounds.

Betty was already dead when he arrived, and he described her wounds to the jury. Her windpipe and right carotid artery were both completely severed, and there were six smaller wounds to her neck and face. There were also deep cuts to the fingers of her left hand, and the tip of her fourth finger had almost been cut off. She was due to have been married within a few weeks and the doctor found that at the time of her death she had been seven months pregnant; unfortunately it was too late for him to attempt a Caesarean operation to try and save the baby. After listening to the evidence and the coroner's summing up, the jury took two minutes to find that the absent McKeands were equally guilty of wilful murder.

Mr Lavender learnt from their acquaintances that for the past year business had not been good for them. Indeed, Michael was thought by his creditors to have deliberately set fire to his house and all of his business records some months earlier, in an attempt to hide the extent of his debts and to avoid repaying them. An action had also been brought against Alexander some months previously for an unpaid debt. He owed money to an Eccles farmer named Mr Cleworth, and Alexander had told the farmer's lawyer that if he could prove he owed the money he would repay it. Nothing had been committed to paper and he must have thought it unlikely that he would have to hand any money over. However, at a hearing on 13 March 1826, a witness was produced who had heard Alexander state that he did in fact owe the money. This witness was none other than Joseph Blears, who had heard the conversation at the Jolly Carter. The brothers had also pawned many items in the weeks leading up to the crime, which to the police officer confirmed his suspicions that they were experiencing serious financial difficulties. To Mr Lavender, this suggested that despite having failed to get their hands on any cash, financial gain

Michael McKeand.

together with a desire for revenge were the motives that lay behind the crimes.

Handbills giving descriptions of the brothers were distributed throughout the North of England, given that it was thought that they would most likely head towards Scotland. It was not long before Mr Lavender received the following letter from Sir Philip Musgrove, Bart, MP, in Appleby:

Mr Lavender,
I write to inform you that M. and W. Atkinson Esqrs, and myself have this day committed to Appleby Gaol for further examination two men brought before us on suspicion of being the persons described under the names of Michael and Alexander McKeand as being guilty of the murder of Elizabeth Bate at Winton near Eccles. The persons of the two men correspond generally to the descriptions given in the advertisement. There have been found on the person of one of them a letter directed to 'Michael McKeand, Draper and Tea Dealer, Foundry Lane, Oak Street, Manchester', a bill addressed to Mr Alexander McKeand, a loaded pistol, five bullets, and a little gunpowder. On the other prisoner, a pen knife, to appearance slightly marked with blood on the handle. You will therefore lose no time in sending the evidence necessary to identify the prisoners to Appleby in order to their being sent into Lancashire, and be so good as inform me of the receipt of this by a line directed to Sir P. Musgrove, Appleby. I am Sir,

Your Obedient Servant,
P. Musgrove.

Mr Lavender immediately gathered a number of constables to accompany him to Appleby, arrest the suspects and take them to Lancaster Gaol where they would be detained until their trial. Joseph Blears also made the journey to provide positive identification of the suspects.

The arrest of the McKeands, on Monday 29 May, owed much to the persistence and courage of publican Richard Faraday. At 5 a.m. on that day William Taylor, a butcher of Kirkby-Stephen, had risen early as he intended buying some pigs. From his window, he saw two bedraggled strangers walking past his house. Two hours later, Mr Taylor visited the local barber, and a constable entered the shop with a handbill giving details of the Jolly Carter murder, together with descriptions of the McKeand brothers. Mr Taylor recognised these as being similar to the two strangers he had seen earlier that morning. Only Richard Faraday was prepared to join the constable in giving chase to the two suspects.

They rode in the direction the two men had been seen walking in, and as it was Monday and market day in Kirkby-Steven, they met many people on the road, from whom they learnt that their quarry had taken the road to Appleby. They rode on for some distance but the constable's horse became lame, and Mr Faraday offered gamely to continue on his own. Three miles from Appleby he saw the brothers ahead of him, and noticed that Alexander was walking fifty yards in front of his brother. Mr Faraday rode on ahead and stopped at the first inn he came across. He told those inside of his intention of capturing the McKeands, and it was agreed the others would help.

Mr Faraday took up a position outside the inn's door, and as Alexander approached he shouted, 'You seem to have walked a long way sir, will you take a glass of ale?' Alexander was delighted to receive such a kind offer from this friendly stranger, and gladly accepted. They entered the inn, whereupon Mr Faraday pounced on his unsuspecting guest, and having restrained him, handed him over to the others to detain.

Mr Faraday returned to his position at the door to await Michael's arrival. However, from inside the inn he soon heard shouts of, 'He's off, he's away', and turning, he saw Alexander rushing out of the door. Before the would-be escapee could run any further, however, Mr Faraday felled him with one punch to the face. He was dragged back inside, but Michael had witnessed these events, and lunged at Mr Faraday, striking him with a large stick as he did so. There was a violent struggle, which lasted a few minutes, before Michael too was overpowered.

The brothers were tied together, and when searched it was discovered that Alexander had a loaded pistol in his possession, and that Michael was carrying a knife and a razor, concealed in his clothing. There seems little doubt that they would have been prepared to use these weapons against their captors if they had had the opportunity of doing so. They were taken to Appleby in a chaise, where they were questioned and subsequently imprisoned by Sir Philip Musgrove, who immediately wrote to Mr Lavender.

When they were brought before the Appleby magistrates, they denied being the wanted men. Alexander claimed his name was Matthew Kirk and Michael gave the name James Carson. Nevertheless, they were imprisoned until the arrival of Mr Lavender's party. At their next appearance in the courtroom, they were confronted by Joseph Blears, and their confidence soon disappeared. Michael could be seen trembling violently, and although Alexander maintained his composure, he looked greatly worried.

Joseph could not contain his anger when he saw the brothers, and was unable to speak coherently for several minutes. When eventually asked if he recognised the prisoners, he declared, 'Certainly I do, they are the men who were at my house on the night of the murder'. He pointed towards Michael, saying, 'But that gentleman has got his whiskers shaved', as he and his brother had both shaved off their very full whiskers in an attempt to disguise themselves.

The McKeands said nothing, and the coroner's warrant for their arrest having been endorsed by the Appleby magistrates, they were delivered into the hands of the visitors. They were immediately taken by coach to Lancaster Gaol, where they were met by a large and angry crowd at the gates, who subjected them to loud hisses and insults. The crowd also made it clear that the brothers would have suffered hideously painful endings if they had been able get their hands on them. They spent the following three months in the gaol as they awaited their trial at the next Lancaster Assizes.

The brothers could not escape their money troubles even as they sat in their cells. A few days before their trial, they appeared before the trial judge, Mr Justice Park, claiming that their furniture had been seized by Deputy Constable Lavender, and they could not therefore sell it to raise funds to finance their defence. The judge stated he could make no order regarding the furniture, but Mr Lavender, who valued their property at £40, agreed to loan them £10 with which to hire a lawyer, and kindly agreed to waive repayment if they were convicted and hanged.

The trial took place on Friday 18 August, with Alexander facing a charge of murder, and Michael accused of being an accessory. The proceedings opened amidst scenes of great chaos; the court was packed, such was the clamour to see the prisoners and witness their trial. The judge had to order one of the galleries to be cleared so that there would be sufficient room for the jury. Initially this was ignored, and it was not until the judge angrily threatened to imprison anyone who ignored him that order was restored and the jury members could take their seats. The prosecution was led by Mr Sergeant Cross and Mr Courtenay, and the accused, who entered the court looking in despair, were represented by Mr D.F. Jones.

Both denied being involved in the crimes, and suggested that Mr Blears had argued with a customer who was refused a late drink, and who had, they claimed, possibly returned later to exact a terrible revenge. However, the prosecution case was extremely strong. The jury was provided with details of the physical evidence, namely the knife, the yellow stick, the stock and the handkerchief, all of which could be traced to the McKeands. Identification evidence was provided by Mr Blears and customers who had been present on the night.

The most damning testimonies were those provided by William Higgins and Martha Blears. William had known Alexander well, and had seen him regularly throughout the previous year. Furthermore, there was a lighted candle in the bedroom in which the attack on Betty began, and he was able to see the attacker's face clearly. He had no hesitation in identifying Alexander as the murderer of Betty Bate.

Martha Blears also had no hesitation in naming Michael as the man who wounded her so viciously. The nature of the crime was such that she was close to him. Furthermore, when she had heard Betty's screams she had picked up a lighted candle, which meant that she had a very clear view of his face.

In his summing up, the trial judge highlighted the overwhelming and incriminating evidence which implicated the two accused. Just as the jury was about to start its deliberations, Michael appealed to the judge to allow him to address the jury members. The judge allowed him to do so, and Michael told the jury that he had travelled widely and had been in places where a good deal of money was kept, but he had never stolen any. He argued therefore that there was no basis for the Crown's case that robbery of the societies' cash was a motive for the crimes, for which he insisted he and his brother were not responsible.

This desperate attempt to save their skins failed, for after just five minutes the jury returned with guilty verdicts. The judge sentenced them to death and further ordered that their bodies should be dissected. The executions were scheduled to take place three days later, on Monday 21 August at 7.30 a.m. outside Lancaster Gaol, at a site known as Hanging Corner. Throughout the preceding weekend, the gaol's chaplain, Revd Cowley, who was destined to attend to the spiritual needs of 170 condemned criminals during his career, spoke to both men. He asked them to confess and Alexander did so, but Michael continued to protest his innocence. He insisted that although he was in the Jolly Carter at the time the offences occurred, he had been unaware of his brother's plan to commit the robbery. He also implied that his brother had been responsible for the attack on Martha and not just Betty. Michael apparently hoped to gain a pardon and wrote a letter to the trial judge, asking for his case to be reconsidered. Mr Justice Park, however, refused to do so.

A temporary scaffold, covered in a black cloth, was erected under the branches of the tree from which they were to be hanged, and two chains attached to one of its strongest branches. At the appointed time, already pinioned and with a halter around his neck, Alexander was the first to be led to the scaffold by the executioner. Once he was in position, the executioner fastened a hook on the halter to one of the chains, adjusted the rope and placed a cap over his head; Alexander turned his back on the immense crowd who had come to witness the event.

A few minutes later, Michael, who earlier that morning had confessed his guilt to Revd Cowley, was led out similarly prepared, and he too was attached to the remaining chain. Both men stood perfectly still and composed as the chaplain prayed for their souls. It was thought that they would address the crowd but they did not do so, and seemed eager to have the execution over and done with. They were standing close together, and this enabled them to briefly shake each other by the hand.

The drop fell and Alexander appeared to die instantly. Unfortunately, Michael's noose slipped and he took some time to die. His breast heaved violently for some time, until he became still and was presumed dead. However, after a few moments he went into violent convulsions and several minutes passed before he finally died. Watching in the vast crowd were Joseph and Martha Blears, together with young William.

When they learned that the bodies were to be made available for dissection, many surgeons applied to the Sheriff of Lancaster. However, it had already been decided that Michael's body would be given to the Lancaster Infirmary, and Alexander's would be donated to the infirmary in Manchester.

ncaster Castle, Hanging Corner

Alexander's body arrived on the Wednesday evening and arrangements were made to dissect it the following morning. This dissection was open to the public, and such was the interest that many hundreds tried to gain admission into the dissecting room. This prevented the surgeons from performing their task, and it was decided to display the corpse in one of the infirmary's yards before the dissection began. After some hours, the curiosity of those who arrived at the infirmary had been satisfied, and the crowd had dispersed, thus allowing the surgeons the opportunity of carrying out the dissection.

Previous page, above: Hanging Corner, Lancaster Gaol, where the McKeands were executed.

Previous page, below: The old Jolly Carter was demolished in the early twentieth century. It was replaced by these new premises, which remain standing today.

2

THE HARPURHEY MYSTERY, 1880

It was the early afternoon of Wednesday 7 January 1880, and businessman Richard Greenwood was pottering in the garden of his home on Westbourne Grove, Harpurhey, one of Victorian Manchester's more pleasant and leafy suburbs. His maid, nineteen-year-old Sarah Jane Roberts, called to him from the kitchen door to let him know that his business associate and friend William Cooper had arrived, and had gone directly to Mrs Greenwood's bedroom. Mrs Greenwood had been ill and confined to bed for several weeks, and Mr Cooper had been a regular visitor.

As he arrived, Mr Cooper had picked up a letter in an envelope without a stamp which had apparently just been put through the letter box. Handing it to Sarah, he joked, 'Here's a love letter for you'. However, seeing that it was for her employer, she took it to him in the garden. Mr Greenwood read the letter as he made his way upstairs to his wife's bedroom. He told her and his friend of the letter's contents, which invited him to a meeting at the Three Tuns public house on Churnett Street, that evening, and which was signed 'W. Wilson'. The writer indicated that he was possibly interested in purchasing a piece of land situated off Queens Road which was owned by Mr Greenwood. He told his wife and Mr Cooper that he did not know anyone named Wilson, and did not intend keeping the appointment. However, he would later change his mind and leave the house at 5.40 p.m.

The rest of the day passed without incident and following Mr Greenwood's departure for his appointment at the Three Tuns, the next visitor to the house was James Partington, the milkman, who made his delivery at a few minutes after 6 p.m. After the milkman left, Sarah went to her mistress's room and helped her out of bed and into a chair. As she went downstairs, Sarah's final words to Mrs Greenwood were that she was going back to the kitchen to finish the washing up. A few minutes later, at about 6.15 p.m., Mrs Greenwood heard a knock at the front door, which was followed by the sound of Sarah opening it, and next, of her maid and the visitor walking along the corridor and into the kitchen.

Meanwhile, Mr Greenwood had walked to the Three Tuns, and on his arrival he asked the waiter if anyone had been asking for him by name. The waiter confirmed that there had been no such enquiry, and he did not know anyone named Wilson. Seeing that there was nobody in the pub, Mr Greenwood waited outside so that he could approach anyone entering. After half an hour, nobody had done so, and he left after asking the waiter to direct Mr Wilson to his home, should he arrive. He walked back to Westbourne Grove and arrived at a few minutes

> Jan 7th 79
>
> Mr Greenwood
>
> I want to take that land near the coalyard behind the druggists shop Queens Rd I will pay either monthly Quarterly or yearly and will pay in advance and I will meet you to nyhlit (from 5 to 6 oclok) at the Three Tuns corner of Churnet st and will tell you all particulars I don't know your address or I would have posted it
>
> Yours &c
> W. Wilson
> Oldham Rd

The letter sent to Mr Greenwood in which the writer expresses an interest in purchasing a piece of land.

before seven. There he found a scene of great confusion and was informed by a police officer that Sarah had been murdered.

After Mrs Greenwood had heard Sarah and the visitor walk along the hall and into the kitchen, she had heard nothing more for ten minutes. She then heard a horrifying scream, and a sense of terror gave her the strength to stand and reach the top of the stairs. She shouted to Sarah but there was no response. With great difficulty, she made her way downstairs, but being too frightened to open the kitchen door, she instead staggered to the front door from where she screamed for help. She was heard by her next-door neighbour, Mrs Eliza Jane Cadman, who immediately went to the Greenwood home, together with her servant, Annie Gillow. The three women made their way to the kitchen door, which they opened tentatively. Although reluctant to enter, they could see Sarah lying on the floor, her head covered with blood.

They were soon joined by another neighbour, Mr E.A. Halling, the district's School Board Officer. He had been playing with his young son in his garden in nearby Watts Street. He had heard the screams, and the Cadman dog barking fiercely. He had also heard the sound of someone running past his own front door, which was quickly followed by a splashing sound. His first thought was that a child had fallen into the water-filled clay pit, which was situated immediately opposite the front of his house.

The Three Tuns, where Mr Greenwood waited in vain for the mysterious Mr Wilson.

However, he soon realised his mistake, and ran to the Greenwood house, where he found the three women standing at the still only partially opened kitchen door. Having armed himself with a stick, he went in, as it was clear that Sarah needed urgent medical treatment. He knelt down beside her, and raised her head gently by placing his arm beneath it. He could see that she was breathing, but within a few seconds this stopped and Sarah died in his arms.

The police were called for immediately. They found no signs of a struggle in the kitchen or anywhere else in the house. There was blood splattered on the floor and on the back door, which Mr Greenwood later confirmed he had bolted before leaving for the Three Tuns. It was now unfastened, which suggested the killer had escaped by this route.

The injuries sustained by Sarah were truly horrific; she had suffered a heavy blow to the forehead and another to the back of her head, which caused her brain to protrude. There was also a deep cut above her right eye. A search of the house and garden failed to produce the murder weapon.

The post mortem was performed by Dr John Pinder on the day following the crime. He found five serious wounds to the deceased's head. One was located to the right side and another to the left side, which had penetrated to the back part of the ear. There was another on the right side of the forehead, and one above the right eye. The most serious wound was to the region

Left: The scene which Mr Greenwood encountered when he returned home to be told of Sarah's murder.

Below: Sarah is discovered in a pool of blood.

MURDER OF A SERVANT GIRL AT MANCHESTER.

THE MURDERED GIRL SARAH JANE ROBERTS. (FROM PHOTO)

Sarah Jane Roberts.

of the left temple, which had resulted in a compound fracture of the skull. The doctor removed her scalp and discovered a large blood clot, corresponding to a fracture of the bone above and behind her left ear.

Dr Pinder believed that the first blow to be struck caused the injury above the right eye, which would have led to her falling to the floor. She had then instinctively buried her face in her hands in a desperate but futile attempt to protect herself, and she had been unable to prevent her attacker inflicting the numerous vicious blows to her head.

The doctor concluded that the injuries could not have been caused by a fall, and were not accidental. She had been assaulted with a heavy blunt instrument with great force by another person. The cause of death was shock, stemming from the fracture of her skull and the other head wounds. Inspector James Bent was put in charge of the murder investigation, and he concluded that the letter addressed to Mr Greenwood was sent with the sole intention of removing him from the house at the time chosen by its writer. Furthermore, whoever wrote the letter knew a good deal about Mr Greenwood's business affairs, as not many people were aware that he owned the land in which interest was supposedly being shown. Also, the writer knew that Mrs Greenwood would be in the house but being ill, would probably be unable to make her way downstairs. The murderer had clearly arranged to be downstairs and alone with Sarah when he arrived at the house.

Robbery was dismissed as a motive as nothing was missing from the house. This included £10 which Mr Greenwood had left in a place that meant it would have been visible to the intruder,

POST MORTEM EXAMINATION OF THE MURDERED GIRL.

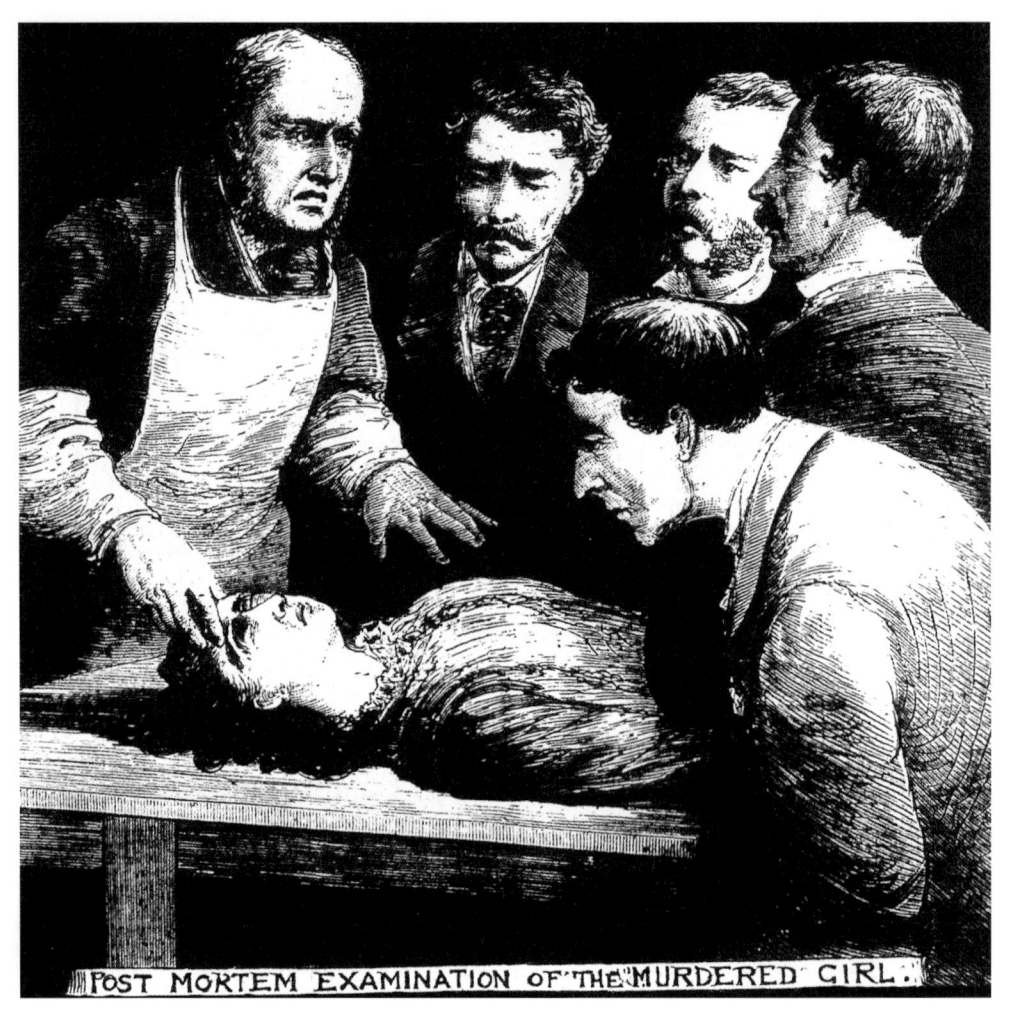

Dr John Pinder performed the post mortem.

who had made no attempt to take it or search the premises. The killer left as Mrs Greenwood called out to Sarah, but if the murderer had intended to rob the premises he would surely not have been deterred by a sick and elderly woman, who could have been dealt with relatively easily. It would appear therefore that the intruder had not been forced to abandon a plan to rob the premises because of Mrs Greenwood's improved mobility that day.

To Inspector Bent, these factors meant that Sarah probably knew her killer and that she had been the intended victim. The murder bore all the features of a premeditated crime, but he could find nothing in her background or amongst those who knew her that provided any clues to the killer's motive or possible identity.

She was a native of Pembrokeshire, and had arrived in Lancashire two years before her death. She had two brothers living nearby, Robert, a stonemason, and Hugh, a bricklayer's labourer; she also had a sister who lived in Halifax, and her parents still lived in her home town of Merlin's Cross. On her arrival in Lancashire, Sarah found work as a domestic servant, and had two such positions before starting work for the Greenwoods ten months before her death.

The New Inn, where the inquest was held.

She was an attractive, fair-complexioned and raven-haired young woman, with a quiet and unassuming nature, and the Greenwoods were very fond of her. However, there was no evidence of any current admirers in her life, and there was thus nothing to suggest that a jealous suitor, or someone suffering a sense of unrequited love, had been responsible for the crime. Other possible motives considered by Inspector Bent were that she was killed to ensure her silence for some unknown reason, or that she had refused to cooperate in some criminal activity, and had been killed in revenge for this.

The inquest into Sarah's death was held at the New Inn on the Friday following the crime, at which the body was formally identified by her brother Robert. Further evidence was provided by the Greenwoods' neighbours and the police. Dr Pinder also provided details of the post mortem. After hearing from Inspector Bent that his investigations were continuing, the coroner, Mr F. Price, adjourned the hearing for two weeks.

A local resident had reported seeing two men in the vicinity of the crime, but they could not be identified from the descriptions given to the police. Over the weekend following the murder, the water from the clay pit in Watts Street was drained. It was hoped that the splash that had been heard by a neighbour was caused by the murder weapon being thrown into it, and if recovered, it might have provided important clues. However, the search proved fruitless, and indeed, the weapon used by the killer would never be found.

It was recognised by the police that the letter delivered to Mr Greenwood with the intention of having him leave the house might well have been written in a disguised hand, or by a third party, unaware of the use to which it would be put. It was the only piece of hard evidence they had, and although the writer had forgotten it was by then 1880 and not 1879, it was the work of an educated mind. Inspector Bent decided to take advantage of scientific advances by having it lithographed, and publishing the facsimile in the press. In so doing, it was hoped that someone would recognise the handwriting, thereby identifying the writer and leading him to the killer.

The police also decided to seek Home Office approval to offer an official reward, and a special meeting of the Manchester Division of the county force met on the Saturday following the murder. The petition was telegraphed to London that afternoon and on Monday morning

Many hundreds attended Sarah's funeral.

the Home Secretary replied, agreeing to make £100 available. It was also announced that any accomplice who revealed the identity of the killer would be granted a free pardon if he or she had not committed the actual murder. The local magistrates agreed to offer a similar amount, making a total reward of £200.

Given that Inspector Bent applied the scientific advances of the age in producing a lithograph of the letter sent to Mr Greenwood, it is ironic that he also resorted to a measure that was based on no more than an old wives' tale. He received several letters which suggested that the retina kept an image of the last thing anyone saw at the point of death. The writers argued therefore that the face of her killer would be found on Sarah's retina. On the day of her funeral, just before the coffin lid was screwed down, the inspector arranged for a photographer, Mr Mudd of St Anne's Square, Manchester, to photograph the deceased's eyes. The resultant photograph was next placed in a magnifying slide, and with the aid of powerful limelight, a much larger image was projected onto a white screen. Unfortunately for the inspector, there was no image of any description to be seen.

Inspector James Bent.

St Anne's Square, Manchester, where Mr Mudd, the photographer, had his studio.

The investigation was not progressing very well, and in his autobiography, *Criminal Life; Reminiscences of Forty-Two Years as a Police Officer*, Inspector Bent described the frustration he felt at failing to make any headway with the case. The murder attracted nationwide interest, and letters continued to pour in from the public with many suggestions on how best to solve the mystery. Several concerned citizens called on him in person at his office, and he particularly recalled a number of ladies who visited him to say that they had seen the crime in their dreams, but invariably they could offer no real assistance. He continued:

> Perhaps before the dreamer had left me, another lady would be waiting to tell me that she was a spirit-rapper, or medium, or something; and then again, although tired and used up for the want of sleep and rest, I had to listen to an account of a number of crimes that had been detected in consequence of what had been heard and seen at spiritualistic séances; till, what with one thing and another, I sometimes wished myself entirely out of the country.

He also received many letters in response to the lithographed letter, which had been published in several national newspapers. These correspondents would draw his attention to some minor similarity to the writing of some individual, which, far from being helpful, proved to be the opposite. Enquires were time-consuming and led to resources being diverted from other areas of the investigation. There were also letters from cranks, which included sham confessions of which the following is an example. It was initially sent to the editor of *The Ashton-Under-Lyne Reporter*, who forwarded it to Inspector Bent:

Harpurhey, February 1880.

Stung with remorse for my evil deeds, and paralysed with terror lest the reward now offered, arousing the cupidity of reckless persons, may lead them to manufacture evidence against an innocent man, I am almost bereft of reason and would willingly give myself up to the police, were it not for the thought of the terrible end I should infallibly encounter. This I dare not face, but I would gladly endure the hardship of a convict for the remainder of my life, as the bodily suffering I should experience might divert my thoughts from their present channel and afford some relief to my overwhelmed conscience. You will doubtless understand from the above that the crime I am guilty of is the perpetration of the Harpurhey murder. To excuse this foul deed, which I now deeply deplore, I taxed my ingenuity to the utmost, with what success you know. After planning every detail of the crime with almost diabolical cunning, I found immediately after its commission that in one particular I had most thoughtlessly over-reached myself, and I foresaw that all the precautions taken for my safety would be unavailing if I allowed matters to stand as they were without proceeding further. To avoid detection by the handwriting I employed an old man with whom I was slightly acquainted, to write the now notorious letter. The thought now for the first time flashed across my mind – this letter will be made public, and this individual will then inform on me. Desperate and maddened I resolved on the adoption of extreme measures. I directed my steps at once to his lodgings and met him on the way on Regent Bridge, Salford. I enticed him down to the riverside, and there – with the same weapon which an hour before had sealed the doom of another victim – I stunned him, and threw his body into the river. Such is a portion of the miserable recital I shall make in the dock if I am convinced that the extreme penalty of the law will not be put in effect against my wretched self, and I am confident that the crime will never be brought home to me without a voluntary confession on my part. I have already written to the Home Secretary offering to surrender myself to justice if he will cause an addition to be made to the notices offering a reward for the detection of the Harpurhey murder to the following effect: 'In the event of the murderer, now at large, confessing and producing sufficient evidence to obtain his own conviction, the mercy of the Crown will be extended to him'. This petition has been disregarded so far, and I believe that if the police are left to themselves no such announcement will ever be made. I therefore address myself to your valuable paper in the hope that some of its influential readers will take the matter up and set an agitation on foot in order to compel the police to adopt my very reasonable proposal. The insertion of this letter in your columns will throw a ray of light over a darkened spirit, will offer a morsel of consolation to one whose sincere repentance and agonising reflections seek solace in the penance of a life's degradation, and will for ever secure to you the heartfelt gratitude of
A REPENTANT SINNER

With no obvious suspect emerging, rumours began to circulate about who might have been responsible for the crime. At the resumed inquest on Friday 23 January at the New Inn, the coroner acknowledged this and gave the three men who were being subjected to such trials by public opinion, the opportunity of clearing their names. These were Mr Greenwood, Mr Cooper and the Greenwoods' milkman, James Partington, all of whom had been subjected to interrogation by Inspector Bent.

The first to be called was Sarah's employer, Richard Greenwood. Many had been surprised that he would have left the house in response to the unusual letter. However, he insisted that initially he had not intended to attend the proposed meeting, and he only decided to do so at the insistence of his wife, who believed him to have been missing out on a good business opportunity.

The coroner asked him if he suspected anyone who might have been responsible for the crime, but he did not. He was next asked if he had had an intimate relationship with Sarah, and he vehemently denied this suggestion. Mrs Greenwood also gave evidence and told the court that there were no grounds for believing that her seventy-year-old husband had been having an adulterous affair with their servant, nor had she ever seen any indications that he wanted to have such a relationship with her.

The next witness was Mr Greenwood's business associate, William Cooper, and he told of receiving several anonymous letters since the crime, accusing him of murdering Sarah. He denied ever having had an intimate relationship with her, nor had he ever attempted to force his attentions on her and been rejected. His wife confirmed that he was at home at the time of the murder.

Yet another man who came under suspicion of committing the murder was the Greenwoods' milkman, James Partington, of Cocker's Farm, Blackley. He also denied either having had an affair with Sarah, or of attempting to initiate one. He arrived at the Greenwood home on the evening of the crime, and as usual Sarah had answered the door, carrying a basin into which he poured the family's milk. He left immediately, and she had seemed in good spirits. In reply to the coroner, he said he had no idea who might have been responsible for the murder. In answer to further questioning by the coroner, he agreed that he had attempted to kiss her at Christmas, but he insisted she had taken it in good spirits and agreed to a peck on the cheek in lieu of a Christmas box. The inquest closed with the jury finding that Sarah had been murdered by a person or persons unknown.

A few days after the inquest there was an apparent breakthrough in the case. News broke of an arrest in Plymouth of two men suspected of being responsible for the crime. Robert Heald, who also went by the names of Robert Haild and Thomas Wark, and his companion, Thomas Laycock, had left Harpurhey on the night of the murder and begun to walk to Plymouth, a journey that would take them eleven days. Two Manchester officers travelled south, and together with their Devon colleagues, had kept watch on local lodging houses. The two men had travelled to the port with the intention of emigrating to Australia and were awaiting *The Silver Eagle*, a government-sponsored ship which was destined for Melbourne.

The Manchester police had become interested in the two men after a young woman named Maria Ellison, who was in service in Berwick-on-Tweed, had seen the lithographed letter in the press, and thought that she recognised the handwriting as being that of Heald. She had met him some months earlier when she was working in Manchester and he was acting as an agent for a cheap emigration scheme. He had persuaded her to emigrate to Australia, where he promised he could find her work as a servant for a magistrate and his family in Queensland. At the last moment she had decided against making the journey. Heald had written to her on several occasions and Maria passed his letters to the police. These were submitted to two independent handwriting experts, both of whom agreed that there were striking similarities to the handwriting in the decoy letter.

Furthermore, the descriptions of the two men were similar to those of two men seen in the area on the night of the murder. Heald's wife was traced to a house in Cheadle where she was staying temporarily with relatives. She had informed the police of her husband's plans to walk to Plymouth, and that she planned to follow him a few days later by train.

Inspector Bent discovered that Heald had made a false declaration before a magistrate on the previous Christmas Eve. He had applied for government financial assistance for himself, his wife and his child to travel to Australia. He had given his name as Thomas Wait, and had declared that he had not previously lived in Australia. However, he had lived there in the past for several years and was therefore not entitled to the financial help for which he was applying to the government.

The warrant for his arrest was thus not for murder but for perjury and it was on this latter holding charge that he was detained. His companion Laycock was not formally arrested but

Robert Heald and Thomas Laycock sold their property before walking to Plymouth to take a ship to Australia.

agreed to accompany the police back to Manchester to assist in their enquiries. Once in Manchester, Laycock agreed to stay voluntarily at the police station.

The prime suspect certainly had a fascinating background. He was born in 1849 and, unusually for the time, did not leave school until he was sixteen years of age. He began an apprenticeship to a printer, but just a few months later he emigrated to Australia. He remained there for four years, and worked in hotels and later earned his living by training horses.

In 1869 he travelled to California, where he enlisted in the 1st United States Cavalry E Troop. He saw a great deal of action in the Indian wars, in which he served with great distinction. He was wounded several times and his body bore many scars. For three months he had the extremely dangerous job of carrying mail from Tucson to Camp Grant, a journey of eighty miles, all of which was in dangerous territory. On his last mission, he was badly wounded when an arrow lodged in the lower part of his face, and he had to ride for fifty miles in this condition.

After his discharge from the cavalry, he worked as a farmer before returning to England in 1876. He began to work with his father, who was a dyer, but he found it difficult to settle down, and after three months he returned to Australia. However, in early 1879, and now with a family, he returned to England, bought a horse and cart and opened a small shop in Harpurhey, working as a coal and coke dealer. He lived at No. 17 John Street in Harpurhey, but his business was not successful, and he decided to journey to Australia yet again, with his wife and child, hence his claim for financial assistance to do so.

That he had left Harpurhey shortly after the murder fuelled the suspicions of the police. However, he was adamant that this was a coincidence, and his wife confirmed his account that their sudden departure was to avoid paying rent on their Harpurhey home, which they could not afford. His wife also confirmed that in order to save more money, he had decided some time earlier that he would make the journey to Plymouth on foot. She planned to follow with their child by train. When Laycock had learnt of their plans he had asked if he could accompany them to Australia, to which the Healds had agreed.

The police believed that Heald and a companion, who was probably Laycock, had been responsible for the murder. It was thought that whilst the other man kept watch outside, Heald, who must have been known to Sarah, was allowed to enter the house. The probable motive was thought to be robbery, but Sarah either refused to collude in such a scheme or threatened to summon help, which led to her being killed.

Furthermore, Heald and Laycock fitted the descriptions of the two men seen loitering in the vicinity of the Greenwood's home on the day of the murder. However, when they were stood in front of the witness who had seen the pair, he failed to identify either of them. This was a setback, but the police remained confident with their case. Mrs Sprague, the landlady of the Plymouth lodging house at which the two men stayed, informed the police that on his arrival, Heald had asked her to clean his clothes. She stated that it took an hour of scrubbing to remove a stain from his trousers, which at the time she thought might have been blood. However, she could not be certain, and later Heald's wife confirmed what her husband had told the police, that it was a dye stain.

Nevertheless, they believed he had incriminated himself when being arrested. He had said to the officers at the time, 'I suppose you want me for the Harpurhey murder, but I have heard nothing of it until last night when I read it in the newspaper'. To the police it seemed that it must have been his guilty conscience that prompted such a response, as they had said nothing of the murder to him. When later questioned regarding this issue Heald insisted that it was not an indication of his guilt of Sarah's murder. He stated that having read an account of the crime the night before his arrest and having heard something muttered by one of the arresting officers, he had presumed that there was more to his being detained than simply the perjury matter, in respect of which he could not believe that officers would travel so far to arrest him.

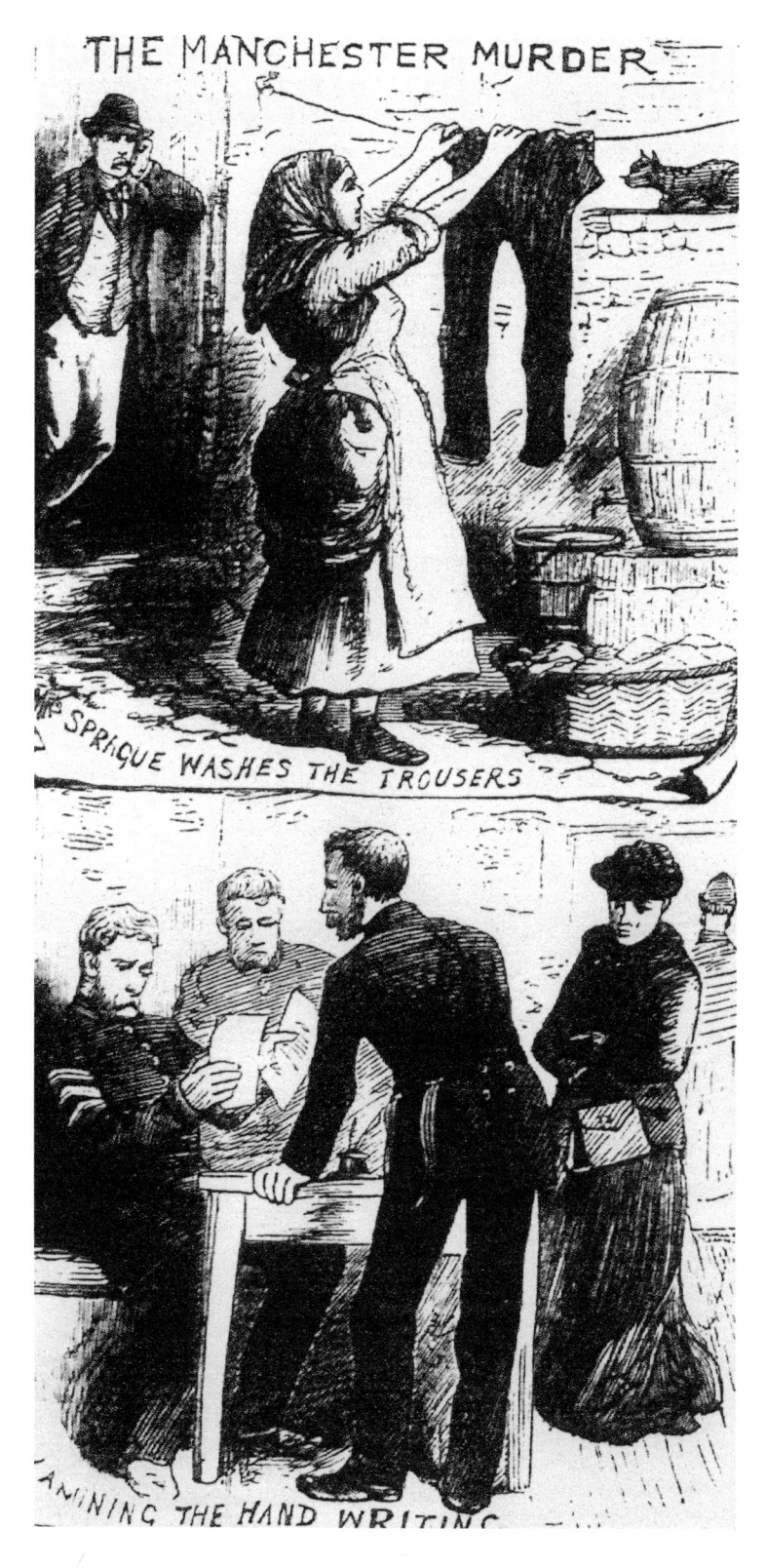

Scenes from the investigation. *Top*: Mrs Sprague washes Heald's trousers. *Bottom*: The police compare Heald's writing with the writing on the decoy letter.

Clearly weaknesses in the Crown's case were appearing, and the case finally collapsed when Heald provided an unbreakable alibi. A friend of his named John Fowsey, of Linton Street, confirmed that Heald had been with him at the time of the murder and could not possibly have been responsible.

Neither Heald nor Laycock were charged with Sarah's murder, and it was also decided to withdraw the perjury charge. On 3 February, Laycock walked out of the police station at which he had been a guest, and Heald was released by magistrates at the Manchester Police Court. Outside, Inspector Bent approached him and publicly shook his hand. There was a great deal of popular support for Heald, whom it was felt had been badly treated, and following his release from custody there was a public campaign to raise funds for the fares to Australia for him and his family, where no doubt his adventures continued.

In publicly shaking his hand, Inspector Bent was no doubt acknowledging that he believed Heald to be innocent of the crime. In his memoirs, the inspector writes that he later solved the mystery and was convinced he knew the identity of the murderer but could not prove it. He made no further arrests in this baffling case and the murder was never solved.

3

THE SWEETHEARTS' DEADLY TIFF, SOUTHPORT, 1886

In the summer of 1886, Maud Hamilton, a headstrong and passionate seventeen-year-old girl, met sixteen-year-old Alfred Smith, an impulsive and highly-strung youth. Maud was the eldest daughter of her widowed mother's six children, with whom she lived in a comfortable albeit somewhat unusual middle-class home at No. 94 Sefton Street, Southport. Alfred was a working-class lad, the son of a Birkdale ornamental plasterer, who was working as a conductor on the Birkdale and Southport Tramway when he met Maud. However, he was dismissed by his employers in August of that year, following a conviction before the local magistrates for allowing his tram to become dangerously overcrowded.

As a result, his father threw him out of their home, and Maud persuaded her mother, Mary, to allow him to live with them. On 6 August Alfred moved in, and it was agreed that he would help out in the house with tasks such as cleaning windows and running errands. The Hamiltons already had a live-in servant, Joanna Pugh, so he was not paid any wages, and instead Mrs Hamilton provided him with a bed and meals together with occasional pocket money.

Alfred and Maud's relationship was extremely intense and they frequently quarrelled, which occasionally resulted in them hitting each other. However, they would quickly become reconciled and kiss each other passionately having done so. They were heard to say by other members of the household that they would rather die together than be separated. In September they each took an overdose of laudanum, but neither gave any reason for this. Their lives were only saved by the timely intervention of a local doctor.

They each possessed a pistol, which they often fired in the garden. They once killed a pigeon and later told others in the house that they planned to buy a rabbit to shoot. Maud had been seen to shoot her gun from the windows of an outbuilding, and Alfred had been seen to point his gun at a group of young men, and at a passing tram, although he fired no shots on those occasions.

Mary Hamilton, who was not the most stable of individuals, did not like her daughter's new boyfriend, and she became increasingly unhappy at their deepening relationship. She once demanded that he leave her home, but after he did so, Maud ran after him. When she returned later that night she made it clear to her mother that unless Alfred, who had threatened to commit suicide, was allowed to return, she would run away with him. Mrs Hamilton relented, but next tried a more subtle approach. She offered him £25 with which to set himself up in business as a tobacconist, but he refused her offer, and Alfred therefore continued to live at the house on Sefton Street.

Victorian Southport, on the Fylde coast, was the setting for the tragic death of Maud Hamilton.

On the morning of 12 November, Joanna Pugh heard Alfred ask Maud to go out with him later that day. Maud agreed to do so, but later she told him she had changed her mind, and no longer wished to. Alfred did not seem particularly upset at first, but at lunch, which he ate with Joanna, Maud and her sister Florence, his annoyance came to the surface. Clearly in a foul temper, he began to torment Maud by tugging at her collar, pulling her hair and smacking her arms. Such childish behaviour was not unusual, and Maud often behaved similarly towards him, so those at the table with them saw no reason for concern. Maud eventually rose from the table, ran out of the room, and locked herself in the pantry. Alfred followed her and demanded that she open the door to him, but she refused. He continued by shouting, 'Won't you give me a kiss?' to which she replied she would not. He again shouted through the locked door, 'I suppose if I can't get one, I can't have one,' and he then ran upstairs and locked himself in his room.

Maud came out of the pantry and sat by the fire with Joanna for fifteen minutes, before heading towards Alfred's room. She begged him to let her in but he refused, adding, 'I will not open the door for you or anyone else'. Maud returned to sit with Joanne, and the Hamilton house was quiet once again. At 2.45 p.m., Maud's mother, who had been in her room all of this time, went out. An hour later, Joanna went into the garden to fetch some coal, where she chatted with a neighbour, Mrs Blackwell. After five minutes they heard a shot from inside the Hamiltons' house. The two women rushed into the house, where they encountered a distraught Alfred who was crying out repeatedly, 'Maud is shot, Maud is shot'. Joanna and Mrs Blackwell ran upstairs to try and help the girl, while Alfred ran to seek medical assistance.

The women found Maud lying in a large pool of blood, on the floor of the bedroom. She was face down with her head towards the door, and she was bleeding from the mouth. She was alive, and the women lifted her gently onto the bed, and as they did so, they noticed a pistol beneath her body.

Dr Albert Wheeler arrived within five minutes and immediately began the struggle to save the girl's life. He applied hot water to her feet and hands together with mustard plaisters to her chest. He gave her brandy, and although she remained conscious for most of the time, she died at a few minutes before 6 p.m. that evening.

Above left: Maud Hamilton.

Above right: Alfred Smith.

Alfred remained in a highly agitated state throughout this time. He repeatedly told the women and the doctor that the shooting had been accidental, and that it had been done in play. He insisted that he had not realised the gun was loaded, and he cried out that he loved Maud too much to have wanted to harm her.

Maud, however, was said by Joanna to have told a different tale. Joanna had remained at Maud's bedside throughout the afternoon, and reported being told by the wounded girl that 'Alfred did it, and he hurt me. He has shot me. He shot once, but the pistol held fire. He shot again and it went off and it hurt me. He threw the pistol at me after he had done it'. This presented a wholly different account, which suggested that, far from being an accident, the shooting had been a deliberate act.

Later, the dying girl said to Joanna, 'Don't be cruel to him. Think of the times that are past'. Maud called out Alfred's name several times and cried out, 'Tell him I love him still'. Her dying words were 'Pa, come quick, I'm dying'.

The police quickly became suspicious of Alfred's claim that the shooting had been accidental, and that he had not know that the gun was loaded. The weapon was not one of those owned by the two youngsters – it was a Derringer pistol, which Maud's mother kept unloaded in her bedroom. It was the weapon used by her husband to commit suicide two years earlier in Manchester. After his death, the gun had been returned to Mary by the police, who urged her to get rid of it. However, she decided to keep it, as she said it reminded her of her late husband. There had been some bullets returned with it, but she asked her son Gilbert to throw them into the sea. He did so, and as far as Mary was aware there were no more bullets in the house that could be used with the Derringer.

The police search of the house revealed a strongbox, belonging to Alfred, which they forced open. Inside they found his own pistol and Maud's, which originally had belonged to Gilbert before he left home to go to sea. The police also found a number of bullets, which could be

ROMANTIC TRAGEDY AT SOUTHPORT.

The crime.

used in the two pistols found alongside them. However, there were also several bullets which were for use only with the Derringer. They discovered that a few weeks earlier, Alfred had taken the Derringer apart, but in doing so had broken part of the mechanism. He took it to a local gunsmith's to be repaired, and staff there recalled Alfred and Maud visiting the shop with the gun. They also remembered Alfred returning on his own to collect it, and on that occasion he had bought a dozen bullets for it.

The last time the Derringer had been seen prior to the shooting was earlier that same morning at 11 a.m., when Joanna was making Mrs Hamilton's bed. As she did so she uncovered the weapon, and at the time, Mary was dressing and she also noticed it. A key issue was whether or not it was loaded at that time. Both women insisted it was not, and furthermore the breach was open and it could be seen that the chambers were empty. If this was so, it was surmised by the police that it must have been Alfred who had loaded it before approaching Maud, revealing that the claim that he had not known there were bullets in it at the time of the shooting was a lie, and that he should be charged with murder.

When Mrs Hamilton arrived home at almost midnight on the day of the shooting, she had been so drunk that she was unable to comprehend that her daughter was dead. It was not until the following morning that she became aware of the dreadful truth. Unfortunately, she was also drunk when she appeared at the inquest, in a crowded No. 1 Committee Room of Southport Town Hall, before the county coroner, Mr Brighouse, on Tuesday 16 November. It was obvious to everyone that she was drunk the moment she entered the witness box. She swayed from side

No. 94 Sefton Street, the scene of the tragedy.

to side, her speech was slurred, and she found it difficult to focus on the questions the coroner was asking her. Keen to establish whether the gun was loaded before Alfred picked it up that morning, the coroner questioned her specifically on that issue. She told him that she had last seen it at 11 a.m. on her bed. There was then the following exchange:

Coroner: You say there was no cartridge in it.
Mary: No
Coroner: How could you tell that there was no cartridge in it, did you look?
Mary: No. I did not look for such a thing. If you had not got one, you would not.
Coroner: Then there was no cartridge in it?
Mary: Not to my knowledge. I did not want to put one in. I had not one to put in.
Coroner: Did you do anything to it to enable you to say that there was no cartridge in it?
Mary: Why should there be?
Coroner: Don't argue the question. What did you do to satisfy yourself there was no cartridge in it?
Mary: Nothing, I never touched it. I always kept it and my purse and my handkerchief under my pillow. I saw it lying there but I never examined it. I did nothing of that kind. You would not dream of looking at a thing when there was nothing in it, would you?
Coroner: (*After addressing the jury*) It is quite clear to me and the jury that at the present moment you are totally unfit to give evidence that will be at all creditable to you.
Mary: (*Sarcastically*) Thank you.
Coroner: It seems to me that you are labouring under the effects of drink.
Mary: Oooh what a story.

Mr Brighouse warned her that she must be sober the next day or else there would be very serious consequences for her. However, she had already done her reputation much harm, and as she left the town hall that morning, a large crowd of onlookers booed and hissed her, and she required a police escort to protect her from even more serious harm. When she appeared before Mr Brighouse the following day she apologised to him, and blamed her grief for causing her to drink too much alcohol.

Fortunately, she had sobered up, and her evidence was more coherent. She was able to state most definitely that the Derringer had been unloaded, and corroborative evidence of this was given by Joanna Pugh. Dr Wheeler provided details of the post-mortem examination he had performed, and he began his evidence by stating that the deceased had been a healthy and well-nourished girl. There was a wound to her arm which was not scorched, indicating that the gun must have been some yards away from her when it was fired. The course of the wound was downwards for about two inches, and the bullet had entered her left breast, just above the nipple. It had the pierced her heart, and the lower lobe of her left lung had also been hit. Her internal wounds had been the cause of death.

Alfred's lawyer accused Joanna of lying about her claim that Maud had accused Alfred of shooting her deliberately. He implied that she had never liked him and she was taking this opportunity to cause him harm. Joanna denied this in the strongest possible terms. The coroner advised the jury that there were two possible findings they could reach. If they believed that Alfred had not loaded the pistol and had fired it in fun as he claimed, not knowing that it was loaded at the time, death would be by misadventure. If, however, they thought that he had loaded the pistol beforehand, this must lead to a finding of wilful murder.

The jury took thirty minutes to decide that he was guilty of wilful murder, and Alfred was committed for trial at the Liverpool Spring Assizes. The foreman also asked the coroner if it

The accused appears before the Southport magistrates.

would be possible to censure Mrs Hamilton. The coroner expressed sympathy with this request but as the case was now *sub judice* he could not do so as it might prejudice the Crown's case. Nevertheless, he confirmed that if the case had been finalised that day, possibly by a finding of death by misadventure, he would certainly have agreed to the jury's wishes.

The jury's attitude towards Maud's mother reflected a growing public antipathy towards her. Many had been appalled that she had been so drunk when she returned home on the night of the killing that she had been unable to appreciate what had happened to her daughter. It was also considered by many that she should have shown better parental judgement and thrown such a volatile and seemingly unstable youth as Alfred out of her house. If she had done so, it was believed that the tragedy would not have occurred.

Alfred next appeared before local magistrates on Friday 19 November and he was once again formally committed to the next assizes. This concluded the local hearings and arrangements

Peel Green Cemetery, where Maud was taken to lie next to her father in the family vault.

were made for him to be taken by train to Kirkdale Gaol in Liverpool. As he made the journey between police station and railway station, escorted by Sergeant Bouvier, several people saw him and shouted words of encouragement and support. One shouted, 'Keep your heart up', and another handed him a cigarette, which he lit once sat in his third-class compartment. As prisoner and escort waited for the train to leave, a number of people gathered on the platform; as the train pulled out of the station, the accused murderer put his head out of the window and waved his hat at those who had come to bid him farewell.

Meanwhile, Maud's body also made a train journey. It was taken to Eccles, to lie next to her father in the family vault in the cemetery at Peel Green. Her journey began at the family home, and as Mrs Hamilton stepped out of the front door accompanying her daughter's coffin she was once again cruelly jeered and abused by those lining Sefton Street.

Alfred's trial took place on Friday 11 February 1887, and the jury heard the testimonies of the main witnesses, all of which were similar to those they had given at earlier hearings in Southport. The jury gave some credence to the accused's story, and found him guilty of manslaughter rather than murder, with a recommendation of leniency. The judge took note of the jury's request, for this very lucky young man was sentenced to six months' imprisonment with hard labour.

4

MASS MURDER AND SUICIDE IN SALFORD, 1888

In the winter of 1888, Garfield Street, Salford was a single-terraced row of twenty-four six-roomed artisans' houses, costing 6s weekly in rent. It faced the site of the construction of the new docks, being built in readiness for the opening of the Manchester Ship Canal, and it became the unlikely setting for mass murder.

Number 143 was occupied by Samuel Hill Derby, his wife Ann, and their six children. It was known locally that Samuel had experienced difficult times, having been out of work for some time, and that he was also in poor health. Nevertheless, the family was well known and respected within the neighbourhood, and the children, who always appeared happy, and who were well behaved, were often seen playing in the street.

Samuel had also fallen out with his father and other members of his family over a relative's will, and matters had come to a head in December 1887 when he threatened his father, Alexander, with physical violence. As a result, Samuel was told he was no longer welcome at his father's home, although the old man's grandchildren continued to visit him two or three times every week.

These visits came to an abrupt end in late January 1888, which led Alexander to ask one of his daughters, Caroline, to call at Samuel's house on Thursday 2 February. He hoped that she would be able to find out why the children had not visited him for several days, but she found the house locked and in darkness. On hearing this, Alexander went to Garfield Street himself. There was no response to his repeated knocking, and he assumed that Samuel and his family must have gone away for a few days.

Nevertheless, he spent a restless night, worrying about his son and his family, and returned to the house the following morning. Once more there was no response, and he became more anxious when he heard from neighbours that none of the family had been seen since earlier in the week. The children had not been seen playing in the street for several days, and the last time anyone could remember seeing one of them was on the previous Monday evening, when the eldest child, Ernest, had called at a local shop to buy some treacle.

The curtains of the ground-floor window at the front of the house were closed and Alexander could not see inside. He made his way to the backyard, where he found the curtains of the ground-floor windows also drawn shut. He placed a ladder against the back wall, which he climbed so he could look through the back bedroom window, but he was not prepared for the scene of horror he would see in the dimly-lit room.

POLICE OFFICER ENTERING HOUSE

Constable Shipway enters the house.

Deeply shocked and in distress, he called for the police to be brought, and the first officer on the scene was Constable Reginald Shipway, who immediately climbed the ladder and entered the back bedroom. There he saw the body of a woman in the bed, and lying on each side of her was a little girl. The bedclothes were arranged neatly, and were tucked under the chins of the children. The bodies were those of Alexander's daughter-in-law, forty-three-year-old Ann, and two of his granddaughters, three-year-old Gladys and five-year-old Florence Helena. On the bed, the officer found a spoon on which he noticed what looked like treacle and another unknown substance. This was not the full extent of the horror, for in the front bedroom, lying next to each other in the bed, were the bodies of his four other grandchildren, seven-year-old Clara Elizabeth, nine-year-old Frank Cecil, eleven-year-old Harold Percy and thirteen-year-old Ernest Llewellyn.

Downstairs, in the kitchen, the by now distraught Alexander found the body of his thirty-six-year-old son, Samuel. He was sitting in a chair in front of the fireplace, with his head resting on a cushion, the upper part of his body carefully wrapped in a brown coat, and a heavy dark blue overcoat over his legs. On the mantelpiece was an empty bottle labelled 'Syrup of Charcoal', and, on the table, there were three other bottles. One was labelled 'Chloral-hydrate', another was labelled 'Prussic Acid', which contained liquid, and the other, which contained a powder,

The bodies of Ann Derby and her daughters are discovered.

was labelled 'Morphia'. Also on the mantelpiece, Constable Shipway noticed a bundle of letters, all of which were written in pencil. It would be confirmed later that these had been written by Samuel, and the circumstances which had led to this tragedy would emerge once they had been read.

The police officer called for Dr William Wilson of Broad Street, Pendleton, to attend the scene, but of course there was nothing he could do, as it was clear they had all been dead for several days. He performed the post mortem on the following day at No. 143 Garfield Street, where the bodies remained. He was accompanied by Sergeant Wilson of the coroner's office, and the two men had to push their way through an enormous crowd that had gathered in the vicinity of what had become known locally as a 'house of horrors'.

Dr Wilson found all of the bodies to be rigid, and he estimated that they had all died between five and six days earlier. There were no signs of violence, or of a struggle. The hands of all the deceased were clenched tightly, their faces pale and placid. The pupils of their eyes were widely dilated, and there was froth on most of their mouths. The jaws of the mother and father were clenched, and their tongues protruded a little from their mouths. The mother had bitten through her tongue, causing it to bleed, and some of the children had vomited. Dr Wilson quickly realised that all had been poisoned. He dissected the bodies of Samuel and his daughter Clara Elizabeth

FINDING FOUR OF THE DEAD CHILDREN

Police were shocked to find the bodies of another four children.

and removed the contents of their stomachs, which he placed in a jar. After he examined these, he found that each contained traces of prussic acid.

The inquest into the deaths of the Derby family was held on the following Monday morning, before the coroner, Mr F. Price, at the Rachebite Hall on St Stephen's Street. In keeping with the custom of the time, the bodies had not been removed from 143 Garfield Street, and the first task for the jury was to go to the house to view them. Afterwards they returned to the Rachebite Hall, where the formal evidence was presented.

The first witness was Alexander Derby, who was asked by the coroner to provide some background information about his son before he gave details of discovering that the tragedy had occurred. He described his son as a studious and steady man, who was nevertheless cheerful and affectionate, and as a man totally dedicated to his family. As a young man he had initially worked in industry, but he was very much interested in science, especially chemistry and botany. He studied these subjects part-time, and following success in his examinations, he found employment with a local chemist, Mr Whittaker, on a salary of £80 annually. He remained so employed for about one year before starting work for another chemist, Mr Brook, for whom he

Samuel Hill Derby's body is discovered in the 'house of horrors'.

managed a shop on Cross Lane. He worked there between 1879 and 1885, and during his time there he became hugely popular with the poor of the district. He would treat accidents and less serious illnesses, and he also performed dentistry, all for little or no payment.

The year 1885 appears to have been something of a watershed for Samuel. His eldest son Leonard died, and he began to experience health problems as he was in more or less constant pain from an abscess that led to a discharge in his ear. It was at this time that he resigned from his position with Mr Brook, as he intended to start his own business with the financial backing of an uncle who lived in Ireland. Following his resignation, Samuel travelled to Ireland, but his uncle had decided not to become involved and instead gave his nephew £120.

The Salford Board of Guardians confirmed, following the deaths, that Samuel had not applied for poor relief. However, his father explained that his son and wife were very careful with money and were teetotal. He had savings and with the money from his uncle had hitherto managed quite well.

Samuel's industrial background subsequently led him into what he hoped would be a money-making enterprise that would make him a very rich man. The railways had expanded massively during the previous fifty or so years, but there was one problem that engineers had not been able to solve: this was to develop a mechanism which would prevent the violent jolting of railway carriages as they passed over points at intersecting lines.

Samuel's attention to this problem came about in early 1887. He was travelling on a train when a fellow passenger put his head out of the carriage window. As he did so, the train passed over a series of points in rapid succession. The subsequent jostling of the carriage meant that the other man's head was shaken from side to side. As a result, he banged his face against the window frame and broke his nose. This had set Samuel's active and inquisitive mind to the task of solving the problem once and for all. He eventually submitted a provisional specification for his device with the patent office. He was led to believe by staff there that there had been many attempts made to solve this problem, but his seemed to be the most likely to succeed.

His hopes raised, Samuel continued with his endeavours until, by early 1888, he was ready to seek a full patent. When he attempted to do so, however, he was advised that he could not, as another individual had already successfully patented a similar design. Not only had his efforts been in vain, he also realised that the riches he had been expecting would not now materialise. This crushing disappointment occurred two weeks before the tragedy at Garfield Street.

However, he had been in a depressed state of mind for some months prior to this disappointment. This stemmed from the dispute he fell into with family members over the contents of the will of his Uncle John in Ireland, who died in August 1887. Following his uncle's death, Samuel had travelled to Ireland, where he stayed for several weeks. On learning of the will's contents, he asked his late uncle's solicitor to loan it to him, together with other documents relating to the deceased's affairs. He did not return them as he had promised and instead immediately left for Salford, taking the documents with him, which meant that the will was still unproved.

Samuel would still have received a relatively large sum of money from the estate even though he would have had to have shared it with his brothers and sisters. This, however, depended upon the necessary legal formalities being completed. The solicitor in Ireland tried unsuccessfully to have the documents returned to him, and having no success he contacted a colleague in Manchester and asked him to retrieve the will. This also proved to be unsuccessful, and Samuel's behaviour and attitude towards his family became even stranger. When asked to return the will and other documents he declared, 'I will burn them first'.

He refused repeated requests. Even though he was the one who needed the money the most, he refused to co-operate by returning the will so that it could be proved. He formed the view that his brothers and sisters, with the connivance of their father, were conspiring to ensure that he received no money. This had been the cause of the argument and subsequent breakdown in his relationship with his father. The only rational explanation seemed to have been that he was expecting to inherit the whole estate, as he was the eldest of John's nephews and nieces.

Amongst the letters that were found in the house was Samuel's own will, dated 31 January 1888, and implicit in the first paragraph is an indication of the antipathy he felt towards his father, brothers William and Alfred, and his sister Sarah Jane:

(1) I give devise and bequeath to my father one shilling, and to my two brothers, William John and Alfred Derby, and my sister Sarah Jane Derby, the like sum;
(2) I bequeath to Mr Edward Brook, chemist and dentist, the sum of £20 in addition to the £6 I owe him;
(3) I bequeath to my sister Caroline the whole of the residue of my property of every description whatsoever, including my interest under the will of my late Uncle John of Magherafelt and Derry Garden, Ireland.

There was also a letter addressed to his sister Caroline, who lived in Eccles, and his loving attitude towards her is evident. It read as follows:

My dear sister,
I hope you will not think too much of what you must hear more or less very shortly. I have made a will by which you take nearly all I have. You have always been kind and affectionate to me, and I wish you every earthly blessing.
Your most affectionate brother,
Samuel.

There was a postscript to this letter which gave details of further bequests and in which he acknowledged his responsibility for the killings (and in which he also suggests that his wife was a willing participant). He wrote:

Tell father I entirely forgive him. I would like you to give to Mr Cooper the sewing machine and such bedsteads, bedding &c as you think proper; also children's clothes &c; to Mr Cooper all drugs, chemicals &c at Garfield Street; to Richard Seery, my late boy at Cross-lane, such of my clothes as may suit him, and to Mr Cooper the remainder. Also to Richard, the bicycle, skates, and such other oddments as you think proper; any book or books which he would like or be useful to him. Also the chemicals &c at Monmouth-street, and two cases containing them. Give something to Mrs Jones of Leamington-street. These are merely wishes not commands. If there is anything whatever that Mr Brooks would like, I beg that you will let him have it. Send to Mr Harrison, solicitor, Magherafelt, the papers you will find in my box in my bedroom. All the other papers of value are in the same box.
    I could not leave my darling wife and children behind. In fact Annie often said she did not want to live after I went, and when I told her a few days ago that I could not stand this any longer, she said she was quite ready to go. I wish our bodies to be sent to Owens College for dissection &c or if they are buried, let the funeral be conducted in the quietest way possible, and at the least possible expense.

Another letter was addressed to his good friend Mr Brook, and in this Samuel chronicles his feelings of bereavement, failure and growing sense of grievance against his family:

I could not go without saying goodbye. You have always been kind and considerate with me, and even much more so than I deserved. You know what happened to me three years ago when my boy, my money, health, friends went at once. My hopes were crushed. My life became a misery. Barely supported I struggled hard for a while against the horrible feelings that possessed me, and I thought that leaving Cross-lane and taking a good holiday would set me right, but it was only a temporary benefit. I became worse instead of better. A year ago, as I told you, my attention was attracted by the railway rails, and that certainly roused me more than I had thought possible, and, so far, a good thing for me. My greedy brothers and sisters have taken care that I should not benefit by it. I have found out my idea was not a new one, and in fact, it was acted upon several years ago by one company, and therefore could not be patented. My dear friends did not know that I only learned it about a fortnight ago. I was disappointed of course, but very little compared with the bitterness I felt at the treatment I had from those I had a right to expect kindness from. However, my bitterness will soon be at an end. I wish every earthly blessing to you and yours. Goodbye. I cannot allow my darling wife and children to suffer more than they have already done.
S.H. Derby.

Other letters were addressed to his sister Sara Jane Derby in Ireland, and his brothers, whom he believed had conspired with each other against him, and he wrote to each, attempting to place the blame for the tragedy on their shoulders:

To my once loved sister,
By the time this reaches you I shall have got beyond the reach of your selfish schemes. Had it not been for you and the poison you instilled into others, I believe I might have had still a little happiness in this world. You can now congratulate yourself on the eminent success of your schemes. You will have done with me for ever, unless the memory of me haunts you. I don't want to preach to you, but if you will take a fool's advice, you will begin anew.
Your heart-broken brother,
Samuel.

The coroner next read the letter addressed to Alfred, after telling the jury that he would omit the foul and abusive language used in part of it:

You may now congratulate yourself and fellow conspirators on the grand success of your plans. I heard your character from your sister and several other people in Ireland, but I could hardly take it in till I proved it myself. You have fully entitled yourself to be called............................
It would satisfy most people to practice your art upon strangers, but your horrible selfishness and greed know no bounds.

To William, in Ireland, who had written a letter offering help in resolving the problem of the will, which had arrived on the Tuesday morning, Samuel wrote:

Yesterday morning I would have thanked you from my heart. It is now too late. My darling wife and children are past the aid of man and I will soon follow. What a terrible ordeal you might have saved me if you would, but greed of money has blinded you to everything. Nevertheless, acting in the spirit of your letter, I will send back the papers.
Your once affectionate brother,
Samuel.

The final letter was addressed to his wife's sister and her husband, with whom he had argued for other reasons. Again he suggests that his wife had been involved in the decision to carry out the killings of the children:

Dear Liz and Dick,
I cannot go without a word. I need not tell you how much I regret that there ever should have been any differences between us. However, if there is any doubt on your part as to my forgiveness of you, let it be removed at once. I wrote to Annie from Ireland to say so, and I should have been very glad to see you, but as you did not come, I did not know what to make of it. You could not possibly have felt more keenly than I did our falling out. If I had thought less of you it would have been different, my darling wife and children are now out of the reach of trouble and storm. I am about to follow. The world has no use for heart broken men. My own misfortunes three years ago and the selfish greed of my relations have made my life a misery. I can endure it no longer. Annie always said she would like to go when I did, and a few days ago she declared she was ready any time. She was a noble minded woman, and a devoted wife and mother. I could not leave any of them behind. They are better off now than millionaires. They have not had a particle of pain. I hope you will not think too much of us. Annie took her dose as comfortable as tea, with the understanding that we should all go, and wanted to be remembered to you all. I wish you every earthly blessing, I am sorry for mother.
S.H. Derby.

Dr Wilson described his findings to the jury, and he informed them that as it was obvious to him that they had all died from the same cause, he had not considered it necessary to perform post mortems on all of the bodies. Instead he was relying on the results of the post mortems he had carried out on Samuel and Clara Elizabeth, which although would be unacceptable today, was deemed appropriate by the coroner. In Dr Wilson's opinion, prussic acid, a deadly but painless poison, had been given to the children on a spoon with treacle. This was undoubtedly to disguise the taste of the poison, and it had possibly been combined with chloral-hydrate to prevent convulsions.

Some of the jury members wanted to hear his opinion on the state of Samuel's mental and physical health. One asked about the abscess he had suffered from, which led to a discharge into his ear. The witness confirmed it was not life-threatening, but it would have caused some pain on an almost continuous basis, which might have prevented him from thinking and reasoning clearly. As for his sanity, the doctor emphasised that he had never met the man when he was alive and could not therefore give a definitive answer. However, he did confirm that he found no evidence of a disease of the brain.

It was important to attempt to establish the times of all of the deaths if responsibility was to be attributed, and the jury heard evidence from a number of witnesses relating to this issue. Sarah Milner had a grocer's shop at No. 147 Garfield Street, and knew the Derby family well. On the evening of Sunday 29 January, she heard the children singing hymns, and their father was accompanying them on the harmonium as was his custom. During the evening of the following day, one of the children, Ernest Llewellyn, came into her shop and bought a pound of treacle. Later that night she was awakened at about 11 p.m. by noises similar to those of furniture being moved. Number 145 Garfield Street was empty at the time, so she knew they were coming from the Derby house.

On the morning of Tuesday 30 January, the letter from his brother William arrived. Samuel answered the postman's knock, opening the door only slightly. At 8 p.m. that night, Samuel visited his old friend John Cooper, who worked at the shop of chemist John Ritson at 44 London Road, Manchester. Samuel had written a will and asked the two men to witness it. This they did, and suspected nothing untoward from his demeanour.

It was implied in Samuel's letters that his wife had been involved in the deaths. However, none of those who knew her believed she was capable of such a thing, and insisted that she would not have been a willing participant. One of those who testified to this was Alexander Derby, her father-in-law.

In his summing up, the coroner declared that, as far as he was concerned, the evidence was clear that Samuel had poisoned his children with prussic acid, and had used treacle to disguise the taste. These poisonings, he determined, had occurred on the Monday night. As far as his wife's possible involvement was concerned, the jury needed to have been convinced that she had knowingly helped her husband, and if they believed she had done so, she would be as guilty as he was. If it was thought that she had not assisted in this way, but had knowingly taken the poison, they could find a verdict of suicide. If, however, they believed that she had been poisoned without her knowledge by her husband, she too was the victim of murder.

Finally, the coroner summarised the last three desperate years of Samuel's life, beginning with the death of his son, his continuing unemployment, and his worsening physical health due to the abscess he suffered from. Already depressed by these factors, the events of the past four months clearly exacerbated the situation for him. This began with his deluding himself into believing that family members were plotting to deprive him of his inheritance, and the final straw must have been the more recent realisation that he would not be able to benefit financially from his hoped-for patent. The coroner considered that suicide was the correct finding in his case. The jury considered their decisions for three hours and concluded that Samuel had wilfully murdered his children and wife, and had committed suicide whilst suffering from temporary insanity.

Samuel's hopes of a quiet funeral were destined to fail, given the interest generated by his crimes. The cortège left Garfield Street, where the bodies had remained until Thursday afternoon, but the journey to Salford Cemetery, about one mile away, was delayed due to the vast numbers of spectators who turned up, and who thronged the streets surrounding the house and the whole of the route. It was estimated that 30,000 people were present, and the police had great difficulty controlling them.

Some travelled on foot, and others arrived in Salford on special excursion trains. Most, however, arrived on special cheap omnibuses and the Greater Manchester Carriage & Tramways Co. laid on additional tramcars from Deansgate in Manchester. The drivers and conductors could be heard encouraging passengers by shouting, 'this way to the cemetery', and 'who's for the Salford tragedy?' Along the route, boys were selling memory cards with mawkish poems such as:

> Their days were like the grass,
> Or like the morning flower;
> As one sharp blast sweeps o'er the fields
> They perished in an hour

Eventually, the three hearses which carried the bodies in eight oak coffins reached the cemetery, and the family was buried together. There was a great surge of spectators eager to catch a glimpse of the scene at the graveside, and many other gravestones were damaged. Eventually, however, the crowds dispersed and this troubled man and his family were left in peace.

5
THE TICKET OF LEAVE MAN, BOLTON, 1890

Elizabeth Jane Holt was twenty-one, an attractive and intelligent young woman who, in November 1890, was living with her widowed mother, also Elizabeth, and her sister Sarah Alice. Her father had died seventeen years earlier, and the three women lived quietly at No. 532 Darwen Road, Dunscar. The younger Elizabeth was employed as an assistant mistress at the Belmont National School, where she taught sewing.

The distance from her home to the school was more than four miles, and it was a journey that had to be taken entirely on foot, as it was over a particularly isolated and wild part of the district, and there was no form of public transport she could use. It was therefore her custom to walk to Belmont each Monday morning, leaving home at 7.30 a.m. as this enabled her to reach the school for 9 a.m. Her route took her along Darwen Road, Blackburn Road, and Longworth Lane. She stayed at the home of the headmaster, Henry Swales, together with another member of staff, for the rest of the week. Occasionally she would return home on Thursday afternoon when her teaching commitments allowed, so that she could attend choir practice at Walmsley church, where she had worshipped for the previous seven years. However, she normally went home on Friday afternoon, to spend the rest of the weekend with her mother and sister.

On the morning of Monday 10 November, Elizabeth left home at the usual time to walk to Belmont, taking with her some provisions and 8s in cash. However, by 9 a.m. she had not arrived at the school. Nor did she arrive later that morning, and Mr Swales presumed she was unwell. She had failed to arrive on two previous occasions when ill, and had managed to send a message just once. Her mother and sister were of course unaware she had failed to reach her destination, as they were not used to hearing from her until the end of the week.

Elizabeth was not missed until she failed to return by midnight on the following Friday, when her mother and Sarah Alice began to feel worried. However, thinking she may have been delayed in Belmont, they went to bed hoping she would be home the following morning. However, there was no sign of her by midday on Saturday and a desperately worried Mrs Holt sent a friend to Belmont to make enquiries. When it was learnt that her daughter had not reached the school on the previous Monday morning, she contacted the police, and the search for Elizabeth began.

The search focused on Longworth Lane, the most deserted part of the teacher's route to Belmont. However, an extensive search would not be necessary, for as soon as the alarm was

Longworth Hall Clough; the cross in the centre is where the body was found, and in the distance can be seen Belmont National School and church.

raised, Clement Talbot, the eleven-year-old son of Robert Taylor, the tenant of Longworth Hall Farm, remembered seeing a woman's umbrella at the side of the path on the previous Thursday morning. At the time he had thought nothing of it, but realising its possible significance, he told his older brother John about it.

John immediately went to the spot known locally as Longworth Hall Clough, which lay a mile from their farm and a mile and a half away from the school at Belmont. He soon found the umbrella, and after a quick search of the immediate area he saw signs of a desperate struggle. Broken plants and flattened grass suggested that something had been dragged down deeper into the clough. Following these signs he saw a packet of tea and of butter, buttons from a woman's clothes, a pair of slippers and a blood-stained handkerchief strewn on the ground.

At the bottom of the clough he found Elizabeth's body, which had been covered in bracken, ferns and fallen leaves in an attempt to hide it. John ran for a police officer, and returned with Constable Hargreaves. Elizabeth had obviously been the victim of a truly vicious attack, for the constable noticed wounds to her throat, and her clothes were saturated with blood. Her clothing was disarranged, and her breasts were exposed. Her skirt had been raised to her waist, and her corset had been removed and lay at the side of the body. Later, a closer examination of the scene of the crime suggested that she had been dragged from the path, after which she was raped or an attempt to do so was made. She was then murdered and her body dragged down into the clough, to the spot where it was eventually discovered.

The police visited the surrounding farms and the name of Thomas McDonald, a well-known local criminal, was mentioned on several occasions, and he quickly emerged as a suspect. Robert Scholes, tenant of Turner's Farm, recalled that on the morning of the Monday of Elizabeth's disappearance he was travelling along Longworth Lane at 8 a.m. in his cart. He was on his way to deliver milk in Bolton and met the young teacher walking in the opposite direction, and as they passed each other he remembered her saying, 'Good morning' to him. After travelling a further

Above left: Elizabeth Jane Holt.

Above right: Constable Thomas Hargreaves.

one hundred and fifty yards he met McDonald, who was walking in the same direction as the deceased, and this was about half a mile from the spot where the body was eventually found.

Robert Simpson of Critchley Fold Farm was returning in his milk cart along Longworth Lane that same morning, having made deliveries in Egerton. He passed McDonald, who was walking in the same direction as the farmer, at about 8 a.m. As he passed, McDonald looked up at him in the cart and said, 'It's a wet morning Robert'. McDonald started to run and overtook the cart. When Robert reached the crest of a hill a few minutes later, he saw Elizabeth two hundred yards ahead, walking away from him. She had her umbrella up and McDonald was one hundred yards behind her. This was the last he saw of the pair before turning into his farmyard.

McDonald could therefore be placed on Longworth Lane, very close to where the murder was committed, at about the time it was thought to have taken place. Other witnesses reported seeing him about one hour later, after the crime was committed. Walter Roscoe, who knew the man very well, saw him at 9.30 a.m. on the same lane, which was by then deserted. He was walking in the opposite direction and as they passed, McDonald called out, 'How do, Walt'? Jane Marsden, a neighbour of McDonald's on Blackburn Road, Egerton, saw him return to his house later that morning. She remembered it clearly as she noticed he was very dirty and dishevelled and she thought he had been sleeping in the open overnight.

As news of the crime became public, the police were approached by Richard Radcliffe. He was a labourer who on the 3 November at 8.40 a.m. had been working on Longworth Lane. McDonald, who was known to him, was walking along the lane and stopped to talk to him. As they did so, Elizabeth walked past, heading towards Belmont. As she passed the two men, McDonald shouted out to her, 'What does't think o' yourself teacher. I should like to take the pride out of you'.

The victim's mother and sister confirmed that she had told them that McDonald had approached her some weeks earlier, but she had refused his advances, and had turned her back on him. The police surmised that, angered by this rejection, he had decided upon a terrible revenge. It was late in the afternoon of Wednesday 19 November that Sergeant Hayward and Constable Hargreaves went to McDonald's home at No. 244 Blackburn Road to confront him. Sergeant Hayward wasted no time in telling him, 'Tom, you are going to be taken into custody on suspicion of causing the death of Elizabeth Jane Holt at Longworth'. To this, their suspect replied, 'I did nowt wrong, but I was there. You will have to get another for that'. He was taken to the police station, where his clothing was removed to be sent, together with a knife found on him, for scientific examination.

McDonald's father had deserted the family when the suspect was an infant, having emigrated to America, and failed to keep his promise to send for his family once he had found work. His mother died when he was four years of age, but before that he had been raised by his aunt, Honor Bann, due to his mother's poor health. He attended Walmsley National School, where he suffered a serious head injury, which his aunt had always maintained had been the cause of his subsequent behavioural problems.

As a youth he had resorted to crime, and eight years earlier he had been sentenced to ten years' penal servitude for raping an elderly woman at Charter's Moss, in the hills above Bolton. Having been released from Millbank Penitentiary on 22 April 1890, he returned to live with his aunt. He was a ticket of leave man, which meant he had been released early subject to police supervision for the remaining portion of his sentence. If he misbehaved he could be recalled and be required to complete his full term of imprisonment.

In the five months since his release, he had had several serious scrapes and had been fortunate not to have been recalled. At the end of September he had been implicated in the death of local man James Mather, who was found dead after a night's drinking with McDonald. Although the police suspected that the latter had been responsible for the death, nothing could be proved against him.

McDonald had been arrested during the afternoon of Monday 10 November. At 2.30 p.m. he had arrived at the home of Martin Ester, his uncle on George Street, Astley Bridge. Drunk, he had grabbed his uncle by the throat without any warning, and threatened to murder him and his family. His uncle hit him once, but McDonald continued to make a nuisance of himself, and he was later arrested by Constable Golightly. The officer noticed that his prisoner had a cut above his left eyebrow, his cheeks were scratched, and there was blood on his lips. There was also blood on both hands and on his shirt. The police believed this to be a simple case of being drunk and disorderly, and he was detained in a police cell overnight. Released the next morning, he was bailed to appear in court on the following Thursday, when he was fined 5s. He asked to be sent to prison rather than be fined, but his request was refused.

Further enquiries by the police revealed that, before making his way to Astley Bridge on that Monday morning, he had been seen drinking in two public houses. At a little after eleven o'clock he was in the Black Lion, a beerhouse on Turton Street, where he was seen by several men who knew him well. Alfred Finnegan noticed that he had several cuts and scratches to his body, which included a deep cut to his finger. When asked about it, McDonald replied that it had happened as he was cutting bread earlier. In the beerhouse he played dominoes with John Smedley, who at one point and for no apparent reason was challenged to a fight by McDonald, an offer that was not taken up.

Later, at lunchtime, McDonald was in the Waterloo Inn on Blackburn Road. There he was seen by Edwin Kay, an old friend, who on seeing the cuts to his body said, 'By gum Mac, th's bin in th' wars', but McDonald offered no explanation. The police believed that McDonald's deliberately provocative behaviour just a few hours after he was alleged to have committed the murder was in order to cause a fight so that he could later provide an explanation for the injuries to his body. As he had been unsuccessful in doing so in the public houses, he had travelled to Astley Bridge in the hope of provoking a violent confrontation with his uncle.

Dr James Robinson.

Following the discovery, Elizabeth's body was taken to her mother's home, where, on Sunday 17 November, Dr James Robinson performed the post mortem. He found that she was still wearing her four-buttoned gloves, and the bloody impression of a hand had been left by her murderer on the left one. All of her clothes were saturated with blood, which indicated the brutality of the attack she had been subjected to. Her jacket was torn and her bodice had been ripped open. Her skirt was rolled up to her waist and all of her underclothes were ripped and disarranged.

As for the body itself, the rigor mortis had almost disappeared and the doctor calculated that she had been dead for several days. On her lower right arm there were a number of scratches, and on her upper arm there were bruises which appeared to have been caused by being held tightly when being restrained. Her knees were bruised but Dr Robinson was of the opinion that she had probably not been raped although an attempt to do so had been made.

He found extensive wounds to the head; two inches above the right ear and beneath the flesh, which was now loose, her skull was broken, and several fragments had been driven into her brain. There were another four wounds to the head, and a small stab wound. There were severe injuries to her throat, and her windpipe and carotid artery had been severed. Dr Robinson considered that death could have resulted from either the head or throat injuries, but clearly she had been the victim of foul play.

Elizabeth could now be buried and her funeral took place on Tuesday 18 November. Her body was placed in a hearse driven by four horses, which made the journey to Christ Church, Walmsley, along a route lined with many hundreds of mourners. Prominent amongst these were staff and pupils from Belmont National School. Special trams were provided, and it was estimated that 5,000 people gathered in the vicinity of the church.

The examination of McDonald's clothes, including his clogs and his knife, proved to be inconclusive. Dr Robinson believed that the injuries to the right side of Elizabeth's head had been caused by a number of kicks consistent with his clogs; he also believed that the stab wounds could have been caused by his knife. However, he could not be certain, and as no blood was found on his clothes, there was no conclusive scientific evidence against him. Nevertheless, the police were convinced that they had sufficient proof of his responsibility, especially after they learnt of a conversation McDonald had with his aunt, Honor Bann, within an hour of when they thought the crime had been committed. She worked at Ashworth's Mill, and he called and asked to see her on urgent family business. As she approached him at the main gate, where he was waiting for her, he told her, 'It's no use wrapping it up. I'm after committing a murder. It's Lizzie Holt. Will you help me?' It is not clear whether or not she believed him, but she told him to go drown himself. As he walked away, he told her that he was going to give himself up. This confession was made before anyone else knew of the murder and after Honor told the police about it, they believed it would go a long way towards securing a conviction.

Elizabeth's murder meant that her mother and sister were left without her income. However, the people of Bolton and the surrounding neighbourhood rallied to their support. Various collections were made, including that by local teachers which raised £1 14s. However, the major fundraising event was a concert held at the local Temperance Hall, for which the organisers and artistes gave their services free of charge. Acts included the Bolton Choral Union and local solo singers Mr H. Taylor, who sang 'Death of Nelson' and 'The Old Chair', Mr A.E. Ellis, whose songs included 'The Mocking Bird', for which he was accompanied by a whistling chorus, and Miss Jennie Frances, who sang 'Home Dearie Home' and 'Angels Ever Bright and Fair'. Also on the bill was Mr E. Whittle, a comedian, and ventriloquist Professor Dearden. During the whole of the evening's entertainment, a life-sized photograph of Elizabeth was projected onto a large screen by a powerful hydrogen lantern. This successful and highly emotional extravaganza raised £45 for the Holts.

The support given to the Holt family by the local community contrasted starkly with the treatment shown to the accused's aunt, Honor Bann. It was widely believed that she had deliberately withheld information about her nephew's involvement in the crime in order to protect him. A rumour began to circulate suggesting that, being a Catholic, she had only given the information to the police as her priest had insisted she do so as a condition of absolution. This was vehemently denied by those involved.

A few days after McDonald's arrest, she went to work at Ashworth's Mill, as she had done for the previous twenty-three years. However, on this occasion she was met at the gate by more than sixty women, who were her workmates, but who greeted her arrival with boos and many unkind remarks. The workforce was unanimous in declaring that they were no longer prepared to work alongside her, and if she was not dismissed immediately, there would be a mass walkout. She was informed of this by her foreman, Thomas McLean, but she insisted on speaking with Mr Ashworth, the owner of the mill.

As she walked through the mill to his office, she was met with more boos and offensive comments from the workers. In his office, she implored him to have some pity as she had done nothing wrong, and asked him to take into account the length of her service at the mill. Mr Ashworth was unmoved, and told her, 'It's all through your nephew, you should not have harboured him'. He dismissed her on the spot and suggested she leave the building by the rear entrance. However, this proud woman refused to do so and left by the same route she had entered the mill earlier, ignoring the comments of those she passed.

Within a few minutes of reaching home, an envelope was pushed through the letter box. Inside were two letters, which she had to take to a neighbour to read to her. The first was an unsigned and terse notice to quit her home, which was owned by the mill and which read, 'Please note we hereby give you a week's notice to quit the house at present occupied by you'. The other letter was a demand for rent arrears of £1 18s 6d.

Facing continuous harassment she decided to go and live with her relatives, the Ester family in Astley Bridge. However, she continued to face displays of hostility. On one occasion she was

Scenes from the Magistrates' Court.

travelling on the tram with her brother-in-law, and a man recognised her. He gave her a great deal of verbal abuse, and would not stop until he was thrown off the tram by a police officer who happened to be in the carriage.

However, there were some examples of kindness shown to her, especially after it became known that the Ester menfolk were all unemployed and no income was coming into the household. There were several anonymous donations of clothes, food and money. It emerged later that the mill owner, Mr Ashworth, had made several of these contributions, and had quietly advised Honor that she should ignore the notice to quit and she could return to her house at a later date, when local passions were not running so high.

McDonald protested his innocence at the inquest and at the committal hearing before the local magistrates. Unable to afford a lawyer he represented himself, and accused many of the witnesses of lying. This included his aunt, for he denied making any reference whatsoever to the murder when he spoke to her on that Monday morning. He accepted that he was in the vicinity of Longworth Lane at the time of the murder, but he insisted that he had a legitimate reason for being there. The police did confirm that he was due to have a job interview at 9.30 a.m. at the Longworth Colliery with the manager Henry Gormley. However, they also confirmed that the appointment was not kept, and thus he had no alibi.

He was committed to the Liverpool Assizes by both the coroner and the magistrates to face trial for wilful murder. He was taken from the local police cells to Liverpool's Kirkdale Gaol to await his trial, and this was undoubtedly a relief to the Bolton police. There was a great deal of hostility directed towards their prisoner, and on one occasion as he was leaving court, a determined effort had been made by a group of men to remove him from police custody and lynch him. Despite his protestations of innocence in court, McDonald made two self-incriminating statements whilst in police custody. On 25 November, he told Sergeant Shackleton that he wished to make a confession, in which he stated:

On the 10th of November 1890 at eight o'clock in the morning, I started from my house to go to near Belmont to see the manager. On my way, at the spot that has been mentioned, I overtook the deceased. As soon as I overtook her I got hold of her shoulder. I asked her what she had been telling lies about me for. I told her that she had set it out that I had followed her a few weeks ago for the purpose of doing her some harm. She told me to let go of her shoulder. I told her I would not do so till she retracted what she had said. She jerked her shoulder away out of my hands, shut her umbrella, took hold of the small end of it, and struck me with the handle across the brow. I became enraged, threw her down and I caused those wounds in her head through being in a violent passion. I then cut her throat, dragged her across the path and down the ravine in which she was found. I made the marks in her neck after making the wounds in her throat to destroy all evidence against me. When I got her in the hollow I took the fern and oak leaves, but before that I tore and cut open her clothes to see if her heart beat. I found it did not. I then covered her with fern and oak leaves. The reason the clothes were so disarranged, pulled from the lower parts, were not caused as people think in trying to violate the girl, as I could easily have done that without if I had so wished to do so. I did not search for her purse or any other articles she may have had. After covering her I did not go the same way back I came, but went over the rails a few yards from the body, went through the clough and returned home along the wall side till I got into Longworth Road. A great many people think the girl was simply got hold of for the purposes of ravishing her but I can swear on my dying oath such is not the case. Witnesses have told a great many lies, especially the milkmen seeing me in certain places. If I had been seen at Longworth Hall at half past eight, I should certainly have been found out that same morning, as Jones came by at a quarter to nine, and that would have been the time at which the murder would have been committed had I been at Longworth Hall at half past eight. As regards the spot where the murder was committed, it was about three yards from the edge of the trail, close to the footpath where it happened. At a quarter past eight in the morning would be the very latest at which this horrible crime was committed.

On the following day he was in the exercise yard of the police station and was accompanied by Constable Cruickshank, to whom he made the following statement:

Man, I had a job with her. When she struck me with the umbrella on my head she might have really run away for I was quite blind for a few minutes. The first time that I knocked her down she got up again and I had to put my leg behind hers before I could get her down the second time. I soon finished her off with my clogs and my knife. Then I took her to the bottom of the clough. I was nearly making a mess of myself as I was part-way home and looking for my knife to cut some bacca. I had to go right back for it and when I went back I found it under her body.

McDonald's trial took place at St George's Hall on Friday 12 December before Mr Justice Cave. Mr McConnell and Mr Steel led for the Crown, and Mr Cottingham represented the accused, who pleaded not guilty. Despite the absence of any physical evidence linking the accused to the crime, the prosecution nevertheless managed to build a strong case against him. Witnesses described the veiled threat he had made against her some time before the murder; others placed him close to the crime scene at the appropriate time; his aunt told of his confession to her; and finally there were the confessions he had made to two different police officers.

Mr Cottingham failed in his attempt to have the confessions to the police declared inadmissible as his client had not been properly cautioned. The judge ruled they had been made voluntarily without his having had to be questioned by the officers, and could be read out to the jury. There

Sergeant Shackleton reads out McDonald's confession.

was thus little option other than to acknowledge that his client had been responsible for killing Elizabeth. However, he surprised most observers by not opting for a plea of insanity. Instead, Mr Cottingham argued that manslaughter was the appropriate offence of which he should be convicted. This was on the basis that there had been an element of provocation as she had hit him first with her umbrella.

At the conclusion of the evidence, the judge advised the jury that it was clear that the prisoner had killed Elizabeth, and they faced a stark choice between reaching a verdict of either murder or manslaughter. For the lesser offence they must be satisfied that there was some provocation by the deceased. He warned them, however, that he was deeply sceptical of the defence's claim that she had hit the accused with her umbrella; it had not been mentioned by the defendant until his confession to Sergeant Shackleton, which had not been made until several days after his arrest. On the other hand, there was his earlier statement to his aunt on the day of the crime, in which he made no reference to the umbrella and had said that he was 'after committing a murder'.

The jury retired for thirty minutes and returned to the courtroom at 6.30 p.m. with a guilty verdict. McDonald was sentenced to death and the judge advised him he should hold out no

The leading participants in the trial. Top row, left to right: the judge, the Hon. Sir Lewis William Cave, Mr A.G. Steel, junior counsel for the Crown, and Mr McConnell, the senior counsel for the Crown. Bottom row: the accused and his barrister, Mr Cottingham.

hope of a reprieve. There was no sign of emotion from McDonald as he was led from the dock and later taken to the condemned cell at Kirkdale Gaol to await his execution.

There was to be no petition to save his life and the condemned man spent much of his time writing to relatives and his few friends. He was also visited several times by his aunt Honor. He met with the Revd W. Pinnington, the gaol's Catholic chaplain, regularly, and seemed resigned to his fate. On Monday 29 December he received his final visit from his faithful aunt and Kate Ester, his cousin.

His execution took place the following day, which was bitterly cold. James Berry, the executioner, had arrived on Monday evening and he was up early the next morning preparing for the hanging which was to take place at 8 a.m. Half an hour before this he was in a side room preparing the equipment. As he laid out the pinioning straps, he realised that he had forgotten to bring a white cap with which to cover the condemned man's face. The press representatives were waiting in the same room, and he borrowed a number of white handkerchiefs, which he knotted together to form a cap of sorts. He tried it on one of the journalists, but it was not a success, and he told them he would have to hang him without covering his face.

When standing on the scaffold, McDonald's legs trembled violently, and the witnesses were relieved to see that the hangman had managed to find a cap from somewhere with which to cover his face. After the formalities of the inquest, McDonald was buried within the gaol's walls later that day.

6

THE DARK HOLE CLOUGH HORROR, MANCHESTER, 1893

On Saturday 6 August 1893, three boys were picking berries in Dark Hole Clough, off Crab Lane, in Blackley near Manchester. There was a sudden shower and the boys sought shelter from the rain under a tree. One of them, nine-year-old Alfred Shorrocks, noticed a parcel wrapped in brown paper to his side, partially hidden under a bush. Curious, he began to unwrap it, and was horrified to find the body of a baby. Alfred called out to William Birch, an adult who was passing by, and who carried the body to the nearest police station.

Dr Heslop the police surgeon was absent, and the post mortem had to be performed by a locum, Dr W.A. Young. He found the baby to be a male, aged five or six weeks, who had been well cared for prior to death as he appeared well nourished and was wearing good-quality clothing. He concluded that the baby had died of convulsions and that death was due to natural causes. There were no clues to the baby's identity, and there was nothing that would assist the police with tracing his parents. An inquest was held the following day, before Deputy Coroner Mr S. Smelt. Dr Young's conclusions were accepted, and Mr Smelt suggested that the body had probably been disposed of in the manner it had been, and placed in the location in which it was found, in order that the parents might avoid the expense of a funeral. The unknown baby was buried in Harpurhey Cemetery.

That would normally have brought an end to the matter, except that a newspaper account of the inquest was read by Mary King, owner of the Temperance Hotel on New Bridge Street, Manchester. As a result of what she read, she approached the local police and asked to see the clothes in which the body had been discovered. She immediately identified them as being those she had given a few days earlier to a young woman who had been staying with her for several weeks during her confinement, and for a time after the birth of her male child. The guest had given her name as Mrs Ellen Allen, and having given birth to her baby on 4 July, she had left the hotel some weeks later.

Following the receipt of Mrs King's information, the city's leading detective, Jerome Caminada, was asked to make further enquiries. Most detectives would have found it a daunting prospect, but not Caminada, who began with a visit to the hotel proprietor. Mrs King informed him that the woman had arrived on 11 May, telling her that she was pregnant but that her husband was away at sea. She asked if she could stay and deliver the baby at the hotel, and the kindly Mrs King agreed to this and arranged for local surgeon Dr Saul to care for her guest during her stay.

Detective Jerome Caminada.

Almost every day of her stay, except at weekends, Mrs Allen left the hotel at about noon, and would be absent for two or three hours. The hotel was opposite the side entrance of Victoria railway station, and it was there that she met her regular visitor, a man she claimed was her uncle. This continued until the birth, after which she remained indoors. During this period she had no visitors. Mrs King noticed that her guest was a loving mother towards her new son.

Mrs Allen left the hotel for the first time on 19 July to meet her uncle, after Mrs King had agreed to care for the baby, who his mother called 'Mick'. The meetings continued almost daily until 31 July, when she told Mrs King that her uncle had arranged to take her and the baby to Kirkby Lonsdale, where they would be living. As she packed, the baby started to cry and Mrs King heard her say to him, 'Hold your tongue, you're going to somebody who does not like babies'. She left the hotel, saying they would be taking the 11.15 a.m. train from Victoria. Mrs King instinctively felt something was wrong and followed the mother and baby to see if they did indeed catch the train. They did not, and a perplexed Mrs King returned to the hotel unsure of what to do until she read of the unidentified baby's inquest.

Mrs King had never seen Mrs Allen's uncle, but her son had done so on three occasions and was able to give the detective a good description. However, Caminada had no clues as to the identities of the man or woman. However, Kirkby Lonsdale struck a chord, as the detective recalled that a few weeks earlier a missing person's report had arrived at the detective office regarding a young woman named Elizabeth Ann Remmington. She had been reported missing by her stepmother and fiancé, neither of whom had seen her for some months.

Caminada thought that the missing woman and Mrs Allen could be the same individual. He decided to travel to Kirkby Lonsdale with Mrs King, hoping that she might be able to identify the woman if she was seen in the town. His hunch paid off, for they spotted a woman very soon after their arrival who was identified by Mrs King as her former guest, Mrs Allen. The detective

THE MANCHESTER CHILD MURDER

The two former lovers charged with murdering their baby.

lost no time in confronting the woman and arresting her on suspicion of murdering her baby. His prisoner confessed almost immediately and also implicated her former employer. He was Ashworth Read, a wealthy mill owner and member of the Royal Exchange in Manchester, who was said to have seduced her and subsequently to have refused to support her and the baby following their son's birth.

She agreed to make a written statement on arrival at Caminada's office in the town hall. As soon as this had been completed and signed, the detective, together with his prisoner, walked to the Exchange and arrested Read on suspicion of murdering his son. Elizabeth's statement was read to him:

I was in the service of Mr Ashworth Read and he is the father of my illegitimate child. He told me to go to Manchester, and I came from Burnley station. He told me to take lodgings, which I did in New Bailey Street, where I was confined, and he has supported me since. I met him at Victoria station and we walked up the steps to Ducie Bridge and then took the tram to Cheetham Hill. We walked along the road to a wood at Blackley. Mr Read soaked a pocket handkerchief in water, and gave it to me to put on the child's mouth. I put it on and took it off again. Then Mr Read put it on again. Soon after he said the child was dead; he wrapped it up in a brown parcel tied up, and left it there. I wrote to Mr Read and received the letter now produced. Mr Read told me it would never be found out that it was my child. He said it would disgrace him, and that he would never hold up his head in Burnley. I cannot tell the date I left the house in July. He told me to write to him under the name Richard Battersby, Spruce Mill, Burnley. I make this statement of my own free will.
Elizabeth Ann Remmington.

When asked if he had anything to say, Read told the detective, 'It's better for me to say nothing'. Caminada charged him with two distinct offences, firstly with the murder of his child, and secondly with being an accessory both before and after the crime.

Caminada was an experienced officer and nobody's fool. Although he had the incriminating statement given by Elizabeth, and this was of crucial importance, he knew he had to gather further evidence. For instance, Read's defence could be that Elizabeth was deliberately incriminating him in order to protect the real culprit, her real lover. She was engaged to Albert Barnsley, who together with her stepmother had originally reported her missing. He was a Post Office clerk in Penrith, but he and Elizabeth had been apart for many months and he could not possibly have been the father of the child.

Mrs King's son was taken to the town hall to see the prisoner and confirmed that Read was the 'uncle' he had seen. Elizabeth had also told Caminada of the places they had usually walked to when he visited her in Manchester. He was therefore able to trace several witnesses who had seen them together and could positively identify Read. These included John Stone, a detective employed on Victoria station by the Lancashire & Yorkshire Railway Co., where Elizabeth would greet Read when he got off the Burnley train. They often walked to the nearby St Michael's Flags, a disused graveyard now used as a meeting place. The caretaker, William Gordon, told Caminada he had seen them together many times deep in conversation and that on these occasions Elizabeth seemed to be in a very distressed state, and was often crying uncontrollably.

Caminada was less successful in finding witnesses who could testify that his prisoners had travelled together with the baby on the day of the murder. Harry Spencer, a conductor on the tram route Elizabeth said they had taken to Blackley, identified the couple as having travelled on his tram one day with a baby at about 1 p.m., but he could not give a definite date. Johnstone Beard, another guard, thought he recognised Elizabeth as having travelled alone on the return route between 2 p.m. and 3 p.m. on a day at about the time of the murder. However, when pressed by Caminada he decided he could not be that definite that it had been her.

To establish the intimate nature of Read's relationship with Elizabeth, Caminada arranged for the letter that she had handed him when she made the statement to be passed to handwriting expert Edwin Reynolds. It was a letter in which a meeting was proposed, and the writing was compared with a specimen of the accused man's handwriting. Mr Reynolds confirmed that in his expert opinion both had been written by the same hand. Although in itself the letter was not especially incriminating, it was another piece of evidence that would make it very difficult for Read's defence lawyers to argue that there had not been at least some kind of relationship involving him with Elizabeth.

Manchester Town Hall, in which Detective Caminada had his office.

The baby's body was exhumed and strips of the distinctive blue-lined brown paper that had been used to wrap it in were still present in the coffin. It was, Caminada realised, similar to that he had seen being used in Read's mill, which he had visited earlier in the investigation. The detective learnt from an employee at the mill that, from his cell, Read, having realised the significance of the paper, had instructed his brother to destroy it. However, not all of it had been destroyed, and Caminada found some remnants when he searched the mill for a second time.

Finally, Dr Heslop, the police surgeon, examined the body and stated that the symptoms of death due to convulsions were similar to those when death was due to suffocation, as described in the accused woman's statement.

Elizabeth's stepmother, Frances Remmington, had been unaware of her predicament until after the baby's birth. She had last seen Elizabeth on 9 May when, unknown to her, Elizabeth was about to leave for Manchester. At the time Elizabeth had said that, following an argument with the Reads, she was going to stay with relatives in Morecambe. Frances had become worried about Elizabeth's health but did not know she was pregnant. Rather, she feared that she might have been suffering from dropsy, which had led to her father's death. It was not until a letter

Victoria railway station, where Elizabeth met Read whenever he travelled to Manchester to see her.

from Albert Barnsley, which she forwarded to the Morecambe address at which she believed Elizabeth to be staying, was returned, that she first became aware that she was not in fact staying there. Frances immediately visited the Reads, who claimed to have no idea of her whereabouts. It was not until after the death of the baby that Elizabeth returned home.

As details of the background to the killing emerged, there was a great deal of public sympathy for Elizabeth. A native of Kirkby Lonsdale, she was a tall and attractive twenty-six-year-old, who had worked in the Read household for two years. Read, a wealthy cotton manufacturer, was forty-seven years of age and owned Spruce Mill. He was married with four children, the eldest of whom was thirteen years of age. Elizabeth was viewed as one of the many such young women employed in domestic service who were vulnerable to the advances of their rich employers. Although Read had supported her during her stay in Manchester, he had finally decided to abandon her in a particularly cruel manner. A public subscription was taken up for Elizabeth's defence fund, and more than £100 was raised.

The accused couple were committed to stand trial at the next Manchester Winter Assizes. At their opening, on 2 November, Mr Justice Grantham addressed the Grand Jury, and described the cases that would be heard. He spent some time on the Dark Hole Clough case and was particularly scathing about the original inquest. He expressed his amazement that no more meaningful enquiries had been made at the time. He further explained that Dr Young, who had performed the original post mortem, was currently at sea, serving as a ship's surgeon. Unless the doctor returned to England before the close of the Manchester Assizes, the trial would be transferred to Liverpool, and heard at a later date.

Dr Young was delayed and the trial opened at Liverpool on Thursday 23 November, before Mr Justice Day. Mr Hopwood QC MP, the Recorder of Liverpool, led the prosecution. Elizabeth was represented by Mr Shee QC and Mr McKeand, and Read's defence was conducted by Sir Edward Clarke QC MP and Mr Overend Evans. The Crown presented what they considered

The Royal Exchange, Manchester, where Read believed, wrongly, that he would receive the support of his fellow businessmen.

to be a strong case against the two accused. They established that a relationship existed between them before, during and after the birth of the baby, and that they had met regularly during the whole of this time. The two tram drivers were called to give evidence, but their evidence was inconclusive. The evidence relating to the blue-lined brown paper which was found wrapped around the body and at Read's mill was, as far as the judge was concerned, of little significance, as the samples could not be shown to have come from the same source and should not therefore be taken into account by the jury. The defence emphasised that Dr Heslop had not definitely stated that the victim had been suffocated. His evidence was restricted to confirming that the indications of death were similar to the cause of death given by Dr Young.

However, by far the most damning piece of evidence against them both was the statement made by Elizabeth. When Detective Caminada came to read it out aloud to the jury, her barrister Mr Shee had a heated exchange with the police officer as he argued that it was not admissible. The detective acknowledged that he had not cautioned her before she had made it, but he denied threatening her by suggesting that if she did not make such a statement incriminating Read, she would have to suffer the consequences herself. Despite Mr Shee's objections, the judge allowed the statement to be read out.

Nevertheless, he later ruled that as there was no meaningful corroborative evidence against Read, the jury should ignore it in coming to their decision. In his summing up, the judge advised the jury that, 'There is no evidence, gentlemen, on which you can safely convict'. Following a brief consultation, the jury returned a not guilty verdict on the murder charge against Read, who was taken out of the dock and down into the cells. Mr Shee argued that as there was no evidence against Read, there could be none against Elizabeth. The Crown put forward no argument to counter this, and the judge directed the jury to find her not guilty also.

Elizabeth was allowed to leave the dock, a free woman. Read, however, still faced the accessory charge. He was returned to the dock but the Crown offered no evidence and he was found not

Barton Arcade, where Read sought shelter from a group of angry businessmen.

guilty of those matters and he too walked out of the dock. Those present in court appeared to have been stunned into silence by this outcome as they watched the couple walk out of court. Nobody, however, could have been more disappointed than Detective Caminada, who was convinced that Read's acquittal had resulted in a callous child murderer escaping punishment. However, in his memoirs he admitted that following a period of reflection, he accepted that given the absence of evidence that could have corroborated Elizabeth's statement, the judge probably had little alternative than to instruct the jury to return not guilty verdicts.

Nevertheless, the detective derived a great deal of satisfaction from the events which occurred on the day following the trial and which received widespread coverage in the local press. Read decided that he would celebrate his new-found freedom by returning immediately to those he considered his peers, friends and colleagues at the Manchester Royal Exchange. On the Friday morning he entered the part of the building set aside for those involved in the cotton trade. As soon as he stepped onto the floor, he was greeted by an angry crowd of his fellow businessmen. He was hissed and booed loudly and jostled as those surrounding him shouted comments relating to the death of the baby and his betrayal of Elizabeth. He sought safety in the office of the Master of the Royal Exchange, but this proved to be of no help, and he had to run from the building. However, he was pursued across the street and into Barton Arcade by a still vociferous group of businessmen. At one stage it seemed as though the group who had followed him would become physically violent, but he made his escape before this could occur.

His reputation in tatters, Read never returned to the Exchange building, and his career was effectively finished. He may have been found innocent in a court of law, but he could not escape the finding of the court of public opinion.

7
A DOUBLE HANGING IN LIVERPOOL, 1904

In the early months of 1904, Liverpool was the setting for two callous murders, both of which were shootings, and which would lead to what was becoming an increasingly rare event, namely a double hanging. There were to be only a further three such executions in the city before capital punishment was abolished sixty years later. The first of these murders was committed during the afternoon of Friday 26 February.

Police Constable Ryder was on his beat when he was told that shots had been fired in a house on nearby Great Newton Street. He rushed to the scene, where a man was pointed out to him as the individual responsible for firing the gun. The police officer grabbed the man, and as he did so, the door of No. 31, the house directly opposite, opened. A young woman emerged into the street and walked towards the two men. As she drew closer the man struggled free from the constable's grip, and pulled a revolver from his pocket. He shot the woman, who fell to the ground badly wounded. The man was thirty-nine-year-old William Kirwan, and his victim was Mary Pike, his twenty-five-year-old sister-in-law. Kirwan was disarmed and arrested whilst the injured woman was taken to the Royal Infirmary.

As recently as the previous day, when he had visited her home, Kirwan and his victim had appeared to be on friendly terms. However, it would later emerge that for the previous nine or so months he had been convinced that his wife Kitty had been having an adulterous affair, and that his sister-in-law had allowed the cheating couple to spend several nights together at her home.

On the day of the killing, Kirwan armed himself with a revolver and made his way to Great Newton Street, where he knew his wife would be as he had asked her to wait for him there. He was determined to confront both women and he was also planning to kill them both. When initially arrested he was charged with the attempted murder of Kitty and Mary. However, his sister-in-law died in the infirmary on 4 March, and he was thus charged with her murder, to which he replied, 'I meant to kill the pair of them. I'm sorry I didn't. I meant it well enough'. He advised the police that he had not believed the denials of his wife, nor those of Mary and her husband Sydney, all of whom had told him his fears were unfounded. He had convinced himself that he was correct in his suspicions, and he had informed a friend, Richard Costello, of the alleged affair nine months earlier. Police therefore had confirmation of the motive for the killing.

During the afternoon of the day following the shooting, the police took a deposition from Mary as she lay dying in her hospital bed. This was heard by Henry Peel, a local magistrate, and witnessed by assistant magistrates' clerk John Dean. In her statement she described the events of the previous day, and Kirwan's unsuccessful attempt to murder Kitty in the house. She next described running into the street after she had seen that he had been detained by the police officer so that could make a formal complaint against him. However, as she did so, to her horror, she watched as he struggled free, took out his gun, and shot her. Kirwan was present as the deposition was being taken down and he accused Mary of lying, and he persisted in his claim that she had allowed his wife to meet her lover at the house. This was denied in the deposition.

Details of the post mortem were provided by Dr Robert Knowles, house surgeon at the Royal Infirmary, at the inquest into Mary's death, which was held on Friday 18 March before the city coroner, Mr T.E. Sampson. He confirmed that a bullet wound on the left side of her body had fractured a rib, and septic poisoning had set in, which was the cause of death.

It was at the conclusion of the inquest, when asked by the coroner if he had anything to say, that the accused once again condemned himself by his own words. He shouted out, 'I plead guilty to the charge, having great provocation to do so'. The coroner warned him, 'You are pleading guilty to a charge of wilful murder'. Even the solicitor representing the police, Mr Trubshaw, felt compelled to warn Kirwan to keep quiet, but the coroner stated that what the accused had said could not be ignored. It came as no surprise whatsoever when the coroner's jury returned a verdict of wilful murder, and that he was sent to the next assizes to stand trial.

By the time of the trial on 9 May before Mr Justice Bucknill in St George's Hall, the Crown had gathered sufficient evidence to provide a comprehensive account of what had occurred both inside and outside of the victim's house on the day of the crime. The prosecution was led by Mr A.H. Maxwell and Mr R. Segar, with Mr Madden defending the accused.

John Russell, a cotton porter who lived on the first floor of No. 31 Great Newton Street, was at home on 26 February. He heard three loud bangs which he immediately recognised as being gun shots. These were followed by the cries of women and children. He went downstairs to investigate and saw Mary and her two children standing at the door to the front parlour. Kirwan was in the hallway with the revolver in his hand. Mary screamed that Kitty was in the parlour and was wounded. John went into the room to investigate, and found Kitty holding a baby in her arms, but she was not injured. Kitty told John that her husband had aimed the shots at her but had missed. She now shouted at Kirwan to leave, screaming, 'For God's sake go out'. Kirwan did so, and crossed to the other side of the street. It was at this point that Constable Ryder arrived at the scene, and grabbed him.

John saw this and informed Mary, saying to her, 'It's all right now, the policeman has got him. You had better go and charge him'. Mary left the house intending to do so, but as she walked across the street, her brother-in-law shot her.

Robert Teake, who worked as a stonemason's labourer, lived at No. 29 Great Newton Street. He testified to seeing Kirwan leave the house after the first volley of shots. Before Constable Ryder arrived he saw Kirwan shoot down the street, but he did not seem to be pointing the gun at anyone in particular and fired at random. Robert went out into the street and Kirwan shouted to him, 'It's hard having a wife knocking about'. He witnessed the shooting of Mary a short time later, and bravely assisted Constable Ryder in overpowering and disarming Kirwan.

When Constable Ryder gave his evidence, he described approaching the gunman and seizing his left arm. He spoke to Kirwan, asking, 'Where is the revolver you've been firing?' At that very moment, Kirwan struggled free, took the revolver from his right trouser pocket and fired it at Mary. As the revolver was taken off him by the officer, having been assisted by Robert, Kirwan said, 'Be careful officer, it is still loaded'. The prisoner was then taken to Warren Street Bridewell.

St George's Hall where Kirwan and Pong Lun stood trial for murder.

Detective Sergeant Whitely made an examination of the interior of Mary's home and discovered five bullets embedded in a cupboard and the walls. Tests later revealed that they had come from Kirwan's weapon, and Kitty had clearly been extremely lucky to have survived her husband's attempt to kill her. Kitty informed the court that she and the accused had been married for thirteen years, and except for the past year, they had been happy. This was despite his regular absences from home, as he worked on the cattle boats. However, about one year earlier he had first accused her of seeing another man, and insisted that she was sleeping with him at No. 31 Great Newton Street when he was away at sea. She denied this in the strongest possible terms and had tried to explain to him that she had slept there on only one occasion, when she had shared a bed with Mary. She also advised the court that she had gone to Mary's on the day of the shooting at the specific request of her husband. This lent support to the prosecution case that this had been a cold-blooded and premeditated crime.

Kirwan testified that on the day of the shooting he confronted the two women as he had intended to do. He insisted that Mary had confirmed that Kitty had been having an affair and furthermore she had stayed with her lover at her sister's home. Kitty, he said, continued to deny it and in a rage he took the revolver from his pocket and fired several shots at his wife and Mary, but he missed with them all. He then went out into the street and as he was being restrained by the police officer, Mary emerged from the building, and as she approached she had called him a vile name, which enraged him further, and this had led him to take the gun out and shoot her.

Mr Madden, in addressing the jury, acknowledged that his client was not insane. However, rightly or wrongly, he had become genuinely convinced that his wife was being unfaithful, and was seeing the man at her sister's home. As a result, he was not thinking clearly at the time of the shooting, and they could reasonably return with a verdict of his being guilty of manslaughter.

However, in his brief summing up, the judge was of little help to the defence case. He reminded the jury that the prisoner had more than once not simply admitted to the shooting, but had also said that he had done so intentionally, and that it had been a premeditated act. As far as the judge could see there was no alternative other than a guilty verdict to the charge of murder. The jury agreed with these sentiments and found him guilty of the more serious charge after only a brief retirement.

When asked if there was anything he wished to say before sentence of death was passed, he persisted with his accusations. He shouted, 'In this dock, I swear my wife is guilty before God. I swear that she is guilty of all that I have accused her. These witnesses against me can say so if they will. They have encouraged it'. This was immediately followed by the pathetic pleas of the prisoner's elderly mother in the public gallery, for him to be released and to be allowed to return home with her. She could not be quietened, and had to be removed from the court before the judge could pass sentence. The condemned man was sent to Walton Gaol to await execution, where he would soon be joined by another man destined to share a similar fate.

Liverpool's status as one of the world's most important seaports meant that it was a great cosmopolitan city, in which many different nationalities lived. It was within the city's large Chinese population that the second murder occurred. In this crime a gun was also used by the killer, and although not a relative, the victim had been a good friend.

Kwook Tim Loy kept a boarding house at 22A Frederick Street, where several Chinese nationals lived. It was also used as an informal meeting place for members of the city's Chinese community. Here they could meet, relax and indulge their passion for gambling. On Sunday 20 March 1904, four men, John Go Hing, Ah Foo, Moy Lee, and an unidentified seaman, who was staying at the nearby Sailors' Hostel, were playing a form of dominoes. Only four could play this particular game, and after Ah Foo left the table, Moy Chung took his place.

As usual, they were playing for money, and John Go Hing was acting as banker. His agreement was necessary if any non-player wished to place a bet on the result of any particular game. Pong Lun was watching the game, and he placed a number of chips to the value of 10s on the table, to back Moy Chung to win.

However, John Go Hing refused to accept the bet, saying that as he and Pong Lun were friends – they should not gamble against each other. Pong Lun was furious and said to the banker, 'When I played you last, you had something from me, now you won't let me try and win it back'. However, John once more refused to accept the bet.

The dominoes were then turned over and Moy Chung won that particular game. Pong Lun insisted that John pay him the winnings he claimed were due to him. John refused to do so, and reminded his friend that he had made it clear that he would not accept the bet. Pong Lun, who lived in the house, left the room without saying another word. Unknown to the others, he went to his room where he kept a revolver which he took with him back to the room where the game was continuing.

He demanded that John pay him, but once more the banker refused. Pong Lun brandished the revolver, and pointing it at John, fired two shots. John fell to the floor, bleeding profusely, and his attacker ran from the room. After doing so, the gunman fired two further shots as a warning that he should not be followed.

The gunman and his victim were considered to have been good friends. John, who was twenty-nine years of age, managed a laundry on New Chester Road in Rock Ferry, and forty-three-year-old Pong Lun worked as a storeman. However, it emerged that there had been some strain in their relationship since Christmas, when John incurred a gambling debt of £3, which he owed to Pong Lun, but of which he had only repaid £1 10s.

Pong Lun returned to the boarding house a few hours later, where he was arrested. He was charged with attempted murder, as John was still alive. The wounded man had been taken to Liverpool Northern Hospital, but when it was realised just how serious his injuries were it was decided to take a deposition from him, as it was feared he would soon die. Robert Davies, assistant magistrates' clerk, attended the hospital with Mr J. Carlton-Stott, a local magistrate, to take down the deathbed

Pong Lun shoots John Go Hing.

statement. The dying man described the events of the previous day, and explained that he had already lost 6s on the game and he could not afford to lose any more, which was why he had refused to take the bet from Pong Lun. He acknowledged that he owed his assailant money from Christmas time, but pressure had not been put on him to repay it. Pong Lun was present as the deposition was being taken, and when his victim asked him directly why he had shot him, he made no reply.

John died on Wednesday 23 March and the inquest opened on the following Friday before the city coroner, Mr T.E. Sampson. Formal identification was provided by the deceased's widow, Martha, who had learnt of her husband's death whilst visiting Paris, from where she had immediately returned. The inquest was adjourned until Thursday 7 April so that the police could complete their enquiries.

At the resumed inquest, Dr Irving, who had treated John in hospital, advised the coroner that there was a single wound, and when he operated on him, it was immediately clear that his liver had been badly damaged by the bullet. There was nothing that could be done to save him, and he died of peritonitis.

Detective Inglis led the police investigation into the crime and had no need to look for any other suspect. There were several witnesses; ballistic tests proved Pong Lun's gun had caused the fatal wound; and there was the deposition taken from John when it was realised he would die. Furthermore, when arrested, having returned to the crime scene, Pong Lun made what amounted to a confession when he said, 'He owe me money. I ask him for it and he said he pay me no more'. Meung La, a friend of the accused, had also advised the police that he had spent much of the day of the crime drinking large amounts of alcohol with him in several public houses, and by the time he returned to the lodging house, he was very drunk.

Walton Gaol where both men were executed.

The trial, which was held on the 10 May before Mr Justice Bucknill, with John Mansfield leading for the Crown and with Mr Madden defending, was something of a formality. Despite the inevitable delays due to an interpreter having to be used when many of the witnesses gave their evidence, it was completed within the day. The trial was also a noisier affair than usual as many of the witnesses took the traditional Chinese oath. This entailed the individual in the dock smashing a saucer and making the statement, 'I will speak the truth. If not may my soul be broken as that saucer is broken'.

The defence could not dispute the fact that Pong Lun had committed the crime, but argued that as he had been drunk at the time it occurred, he could not have been in full possession of his faculties, and he could not have formed an intent to kill his victim. Thus, it was argued, in these circumstances, a verdict of manslaughter was the most appropriate. In his summing up of the evidence, the judge advised the jury that being drunk was no defence, and based on the evidence that had been presented, he could see no other verdict than wilful murder being appropriate. The jury agreed, for without leaving their seats they returned that verdict. As the judge was sentencing the prisoner to death, Mrs Go Hing began to cry loudly and screamed, 'Oh my fatherless child', before fainting.

There were to be no successful petitions to spare the two condemned men, and it was arranged that they would be executed simultaneously on Tuesday 31 May, at Walton Gaol. Both of the condemned awaited their appointment with the hangman, William Billington, with equanimity. Kirwan spent much of the time he had left with Father Brown, the gaol's Catholic priest, and Pong Lun, who converted to Christianity whilst in the condemned cell, was confirmed by the Bishop of Liverpool on the Sunday before his execution.

On the eve of the hangings, Kirwan received a final visit from his brother and sister. Pong Lun was visited by a friend, but he refused to meet Miss Parslow, a well-known Chinese missionary who had interested herself in the case and who presented herself at the gaol's gates. At 8 a.m. the following day the two men stood side by side on the gallows and met their ends stoically.

8

THE YORKSHIRE STREET ROBBERY, OLDHAM, 1913

At 10 p.m. on Saturday 26 July 1913, stationer and bookseller Daniel Wright Bardsley was closing his shop at 43 Yorkshire Street, Oldham. It was a successful business and he employed three members of staff: Edward Hilton, Annie Leach and Clara Hall. The young man had locked the front door to the premises, and Annie had counted out the day's takings. She left £1 in the till, ready for the next day's business, and handed the rest of the takings, which totalled £3, to Mr Bardsley.

Mr Bardsley told Annie that he intended writing a letter that night to a young man he wished to employ instead of Hilton as he was going to dismiss him, and that he would be giving him one week's notice that night before he went home. Hilton had been working at the shop for three weeks, but he had not performed his duties, which had included sweeping up, cleaning windows, packing and running errands, to a sufficiently high standard.

Mr Bardsley, true to his word, gave Hilton one week's notice a few minutes later, and a disconsolate young man left the shop soon afterwards. Twenty minutes later, Annie and Clara left together by the back door, which remained unlocked. Mr Bardsley was now left alone in the shop, as it was his habit to complete his accounts before going home, meaning he would often work until well into the early hours of the morning. A bachelor of fifty-four, he had lived with his brother John at 89 Egerton Street for fifteen years.

Five hours after Annie and Clara had left the shop, James Greaves, a nightwatchman with the privately operated Yorkshire Street Watch, inspected the back of Mr Bardsley's shop. All was in darkness, but he noticed that the gate leading into the backyard was open. His suspicions aroused, he approached the door that led into the rear room of the shop, and found it to be unlocked. He pushed against it, but it would open only a few inches, as something was blocking it. He pushed harder and managed to create enough space for him to enter the room. Once in the room he turned up the light of his lantern, and was horrified to discover that it was the body of Mr Bardsley that was causing the difficulty. It was obvious that he was dead and beyond help, and he rushed to the town hall to inform the police.

They found the body lying in a large pool of blood on the floor. The clothing on the upper part of his body was saturated with blood. His head and face showed signs of a savage beating, and were also covered in blood, as was his arm, with which he had attempted to defend himself. All of his waistcoat buttons were unfastened, as though a search of his clothing had been made.

Yorkshire Street.

    Four keys lay to the left of the body, and a number of letters were scattered about the floor. Also close to the body there lay a large Indian club, which bore traces of blood and hair. Upstairs, the police examined the safe, which was locked, but which showed signs of an unsuccessful attempt having been made to open it with a chisel or similar implement.

    The body was taken to the mortuary at 5 a.m., and a post mortem was performed by Dr A. Jackson, pathologist at Oldham Royal Infirmary, on the Sunday afternoon. He found a deep wound one and a half inches long at the point of the chin. There were several abrasions and bruises above both eyes, and he found a large bruise on the back of the head. There were several extensive fractures of the skull, as though it had been hit savagely on its top and base. Blood had escaped from the left ear, and blood had also accumulated in the nose and mouth. Dr Jackson concluded that death had resulted from a fractured skull, and that the victim had been hit on the head at least twice with great force. He concluded that the Indian club found at the scene of the crime was undoubtedly the blunt instrument used to commit the murder.

    The police interviewed Annie and Clara, and as a result of these enquiries, they focused their investigation on Edward Wilde Hilton, the youth who had been given one week's notice by the dead man. He was thought to be eighteen years old, but he was one year younger, and later this would prove to be of huge significance. They visited him at home, and when asked to give an account of his movements he gave a rather bizarre explanation, which simply added to their suspicions. He denied any involvement in the murder, and insisted that he had left the shop at 9.45 p.m. He had then travelled to Hollinwood Wakes with a friend. However, although he had known this friend for about three months he did not know his name. He had returned home at about midnight.

Daniel Bardsley's shop.

Not surprisingly, this did not satisfy the police, who conducted a search of his home. They found a pair of socks and a pair of trousers on which were found what were clearly blood stains. When they searched his clothing they found a two shilling piece, two silver shillings, and a penny. Later, following further questioning, Hilton admitted that he had been involved in the robbery, but he denied murdering the victim. He placed the blame on the friend he had initially failed to name, but who he now identified as twenty-year-old Ernest Edwin Kelly, who lived at 119 Ward Street.

The police immediately went to Kelly's home, and the young man said, 'Well, come into the front room. Don't let my mother hear you'. Later he told them, 'I will show you where I put all I got'. He led the officers into the backyard, and buried near to the privy they found 9s 6d in silver, some copper and four keys.

Also buried were four gold signet rings, which would later prove to be particularly important pieces of evidence. On the day of the murder, Mr Bardsley had sent Clara to Hirsts, a local jeweller's, to bring six of these rings for him to view on approval. Clara and Annie last saw them just as they were leaving the shop on the night of the crime, as their employer was putting the rings in his waistcoat pocket. Before they left Kelly's home, the police searched amongst his clothes and found a pair of blood-soaked socks and a coat which also had traces of blood on it.

When he heard of these developments, Hilton decided to lead the police to Painter Street, where, it emerged, he had buried his share of the robbery. He put his hand in a hole in the wall and pulled out 25s in silver wrapped in a handkerchief, a few pennies, and more significantly, the two remaining gold signet rings.

The police decided that they had enough evidence to charge both of the suspects with the murder. When asked if they had anything to say, Kelly replied, 'Guilty for me. I hit him with the club and then threw it down. Hilton hit him twice and then went upstairs'. Hilton, however, gave a significantly different response, for he replied, 'Not guilty. I never touched him with a club. I never touched him with anything. I gave him a drink of water. That's all'.

They each therefore gave conflicting versions of what had occurred from the very start of the case, and these would be the focus of the trial which was to be held at the next Manchester Assizes. As the two accused awaited their trial, arrangements were made to bury Mr Bardsley. He was a native of Oldham, and had attended St Peter's Church School as a boy. He left when he was thirteen years old and, being a bright pupil, he immediately started work for a local stationer, where he remained for the next twenty years, before eventually becoming shop manager. When this business closed down, he decided to open his own shop. His first shop was at 34 Yorkshire Street, but as his business expanded, he moved to the larger premises, where he met his death. A pleasant and jovial man, he was well known throughout the town, and not simply because of his business interests. He was keen on amateur dramatics, and was closely associated with the Oldham Lyceum, and he had also sponsored several shows at the Grand Theatre.

Mr Bardsley was buried at Greenacres Cemetery during the afternoon of Thursday 31 July. The cortège, which included ten coaches for family and friends, left 89 Egerton Street and travelled to the Salem Moravian church, at which he had worshipped regularly for many years. In keeping with local custom, the blinds and curtains of the houses and businesses along the route were closed as a mark of respect. At the small church, the service was led by his good friends, the Revds W. Sitterington and C.J. Shaw. There were emotional scenes throughout the service, but his long-serving assistant Annie Leach was especially distressed and had to be supported by friends.

There were many wreaths, amongst which was one from Hilton's parents. Attached to it was a card, written on which were the words, 'What I do now thou knowest not; thou shalt

THE OLDHAM MURDER

The Prisoners Give Evidence

Mutual Recriminations

GHASTLY GRAPHIC STORIES

THE SCENE IN THE SHOP

MR. BARDSLEY CONSCIOUS DURING ATTACK

Details of the horrific murder appear in the local press.

know hereafter'. No doubt these sentiments reflected their own struggle to find some kind of explanation for the events of the previous few days, which had had such a devastating impact on their own family.

The trial of the two accused took place on Monday 24 November at the Manchester Assizes, before Mr Justice Avory. The prosecution was led by Gordon Hewart, who was assisted by Mr Henriques. The defence barrister for Kelly was Mr Ryecroft, and Mr Cleary represented Hilton. That both had been present in Mr Bardsley's shop when the robbery and murder occurred was acknowledged by both defence teams. However, Kelly and Hilton had provided differing accounts as to what had occurred in their respective statements to the police, and at the trial they would each place the blame on the other for the murder itself. This led Mr Cleary to ask the judge to consider holding separate trials, but this request was refused.

Kelly told the court that he and Hilton had arranged to meet at 9.50 p.m. at the front of Mr Bardsley's shop on the night in question, and they planned to make their way to Hollinwood Wakes. However, when they met, Hilton told him that he was to be sacked, and suggested that they rob his employer. Hilton gave Kelly 6d to take the tram to his home and collect his Indian club, which they could use as a weapon. Kelly insisted that he understood that it would be used only to threaten Mr Bardsley with, and not to beat or kill him.

It had taken Kelly no more than a few minutes to return with the club, and he went to the yard at the rear of the shop, where the two of them hid until the two female assistants left the premises. Before entering the shop both youths took off their boots so they would not be heard. Once inside, they hid and saw Mr Bardsley lock the back door before going upstairs. Hilton then suggested to Kelly that they exchange coats, as he believed this would make it more difficult for their victim to recognise him. Hilton also suggested that Kelly use the club as Hilton might hit him too hard.

The older man eventually came downstairs, and Hilton, his face partially covered and in a disguised voice, shouted 'Hands up'. A startled Mr Bardsley tried to run out of the room, but in his panic, he fell to the floor. Kelly admitted that at this point he hit him with the club, but only on the shoulder. Kelly said that he then threw the club to the ground and turned the injured man on to his back to check on his condition. He was conscious but blood was flowing from his nose. It was then that Hilton is said to have picked the club up and hit Mr Bardsley, a savage blow to the head. Hilton next began to search through Mr Bardsley's pockets, and Kelly joined in doing so also. Kelly said that he removed 2s and Hilton removed more money and some keys. Kelly then discovered the six gold signet rings.

Kelly next saw Hilton going to the front of the shop and heard him emptying the till. Hilton then went upstairs and was unsuccessful in his attempts to open the safe with the keys he had found on Mr Bardsley. He tried to force it open with a screwdriver, but failed to do so. Kelly had followed him, and continued to try and open the safe after Hilton went downstairs. Kelly was forced to give up, and on reaching downstairs, he was told by Hilton that he had given the injured man a drink of water. Kelly suggested they wipe his face before they left, and he did so with a damp cloth.

The pair left the shop, and Kelly insisted that Mr Bardsley was still alive when they did so. Hilton told his accomplice that he had forgotten something and he went back into the shop on his own, where he remained for several minutes. When Hilton emerged from the building, they fled the scene and divided the takings, before each made their way home.

Hilton gave a very different version of events. After stating that he had known Kelly for about three months before the crime, and that they would often go to the cinema or simply walk about the streets, he agreed that they had arranged to meet with the intention of attending Hollinwood Wakes. However, Hilton insisted that he did not meet his friend at the front of the shop, where he usually waited, as Kelly had stated. Instead, Kelly had appeared in the backyard and asked if there was any money on the premises. On hearing that there was, Kelly said 'We'll attack him'.

According to Hilton, he replied, 'No, we'll wait until Mr Bardsley has gone home'. Kelly borrowed 6d and said he would go home, but again Hilton insisted that he did not know why at this stage, and that when Kelly did return, he had not seen the Indian club. The pair waited outside until Annie and Clara left.

Hilton emphasised that when he entered the shop at this stage, it was not with any intention of committing a robbery, nor was he expecting Kelly to follow him in. He insisted that he had returned only to collect his apron, which he had forgotten when he left earlier that evening. Once inside, Hilton encountered Mr Bardsley, who is said to have agreed to let him go into another room for his apron. When he was doing so, he heard the older man cry out. Hilton rushed into that room to see him falling to the floor with Kelly standing above him with the Indian club in his hand.

He described Mr Bardsley trying to push himself up, only to be hit savagely once again by Kelly, this time to the left side of the face. Kelly made as though to hit him once more, but Hilton insisted that he cried out, 'Don't, God will punish us if you hit him again'. Kelly dropped the club, and Mr Bardsley tried once again to raise himself, and as he did so, he touched Hilton. This, Hilton suggested, is how the victim's blood came to be on his clothes.

The two youths are said to have gone to the safe, which was upstairs, to see if it was open. Hilton described hearing their victim groaning, so he went downstairs and gave him a glass of water. At this point, Kelly approached, and despite Hilton's protests, he once again hit the man violently to the head. Kelly then told Hilton to find a cloth, with which Kelly wiped the man's face, before screwing it up tightly and putting it in Mr Bardsley's mouth. The pair then searched through the man's pockets and found the letters, some money, and the six gold signet rings. They also found the keys with which they tried unsuccessfully to open the safe, and which they also failed to achieve by using a screwdriver. Kelly gave Hilton 2s, and two of the rings. Hilton was adamant that he had not hit Mr Bardsley, and that Kelly had struck all of the blows.

In his summing up to the jury, the judge focused almost entirely on these two conflicting versions of events provided by the two unsophisticated and inarticulate youths, each of whom was attempting to blame the other for the murder of Mr Bardsley. He emphasised that if two individuals agree together to commit a crime, in this case robbery, and in order to carry out this common purpose violence is used which could lead to death or to grievous bodily harm being caused, both are guilty of murder even if the violence is committed by just one of them.

The jury retired for twenty-five minutes before returning with guilty verdicts in respect of both of the accused. However, they recommended mercy for both in view of their youth. Kelly and Hilton stood impassively in the dock as the judge told them:

> You are young to die the degrading death which by law you are now subject to. It lies not with me either to express any opinion or to hold out any hope to you as to the effect of the recommendation of the jury. It will be forwarded to the proper quarter. You hurried your victim to eternity without giving him time to make any preparations to meet his maker. The law is more merciful to you; it gives you that time.

He then passed sentences of death on both of them, having first placed the traditional black cap on his head. These sentences prompted an immediate campaign to obtain reprieves for both young men. A joint petition signed by 20,000 people emphasised the youth of both and the absence of any previous convictions. Many of Oldham's leading citizens supported the campaign, including Mrs Alderman Lees, a former mayor, who wrote to the local press that, 'Reprieve does not mean pardon, and although a feeble minded youth like Hilton, and one so easily led as Kelly are not fit to have their liberty, neither should be hanged, and I shall sign the petition'.

However, the campaign proved to be only partially successful. The Home Secretary was not persuaded that both should be spared, and the decision was made that only Hilton was to be reprieved. The different manner in which each was treated caused outrage in the town. There were spontaneous protests throughout Oldham on Monday 15 December, the day the Home Secretary's decision became known. The Oldham Labour Party sent a telegram to the Home Office, protesting against the decision. A mass meeting of the employees of Messrs Platt Bros, where Kelly had been employed, was held in his support. Oldham Education Committee sent a letter of protest, and a similar letter was sent to the Home Secretary by those who attended a meeting held at the local Salvation Army Hall. Also, throughout the day, groups of disgruntled people gathered outside the town hall.

A public meeting was arranged hurriedly for 8 p.m. that night at the town hall, and by that time a crowd of 50,000 had assembled. They were addressed from an upper window by the mayor, Alderman Wilde, who had to use a megaphone to make himself heard. He confirmed that local Members of Parliament had petitioned the Home Secretary personally, but had been unsuccessful. He proposed that the following petition be sent:

That this public meeting of inhabitants of Oldham is strongly of the opinion that in as much as the death sentence passed on Edward Wild Hilton, one of the prisoners found guilty of the murder of Daniel Wright Bardsley, at Oldham, has been respited, the same clemency also ought to be extended to Ernest Edwin Kelly, the other prisoner, and earnestly hopes that the Secretary of State will be able to give effect to this recommendation.

Furthermore, the meeting decided to send a delegation of six to the Home Office the following day, and these were the mayor, the chief constable, the town clerk, Kelly's solicitor and two representatives of local trade unions, Mr W. Mullin and Mr J. Grinion.

The Secretary of State declined to meet them on their arrival in London, and in his place they met with one of his officials. The Home Secretary was not persuaded to change his mind, and on the morning of Wednesday 17 December, news reached the town that they had failed to save Kelly from the hangman's noose, and that his execution would go ahead at Strangeways Gaol at 8 a.m. the following morning.

As the execution drew closer, the mayoress sent a telegram to the Queen asking for her support, which seemed to represent accurately the feelings of many local residents. It read as follows:

May I approach your Majesty to assist in our endeavour to obtain a reprieve for Kelly, one of the Oldham murderers, who is to be executed tomorrow morning. Hilton, the other prisoner, has been reprieved, and great indignation has been aroused by the decision of the Home Secretary not to treat both prisoners alike. The public feel that the least guilty of the two is to hang.

Later that day, Kelly met with his parents, his brother and his sister-in-law, together with his sister, for a final and highly emotional meeting, which lasted for one hour.

Thirty thousand people again assembled outside the town hall that night, and the mood was by now extremely ugly. By 9.30 p.m. the town centre was packed with a swaying and vociferous crowd, which prevented the movement of any traffic. Mounted police were hurriedly called for to try and restore order. At 10.30 p.m. Alderman Isherwood appeared at a town hall window, and there was a loud cheer as the crowd presumed it was good news he was going to give them. However, when they realised that there was to be no reprieve, the crowd became even more disorderly. Abusive comments about the Home Secretary were heard, and at a few minutes after midnight, a large section of the crowd marched down Manchester Street, throwing stones and smashing the windows of several passing trams. They next turned their attention to the police station, which was attacked and which had many windows broken.

When it became obvious that almost 10,000 people were determined to march to Strangeways Gaol, where 4,000 angry demonstrators were already gathered, the police began to fear there would be serious public disorder. Arrangements were quickly made for several hundred police to patrol the area surrounding the gaol to prevent massive displays of protest. The first party to arrive from Oldham in the early hours comprised about 500 demonstrators; many carried torch lights and, more worryingly, many were armed with heavy sticks, pokers and other iron bars. They sang and shouted defiantly, and prominent in the crowd were many women who wore their shawls to protect them against the severe cold weather.

There was a confrontation with the police near to the gaol gates, and the crowd was warned not to cause any further trouble and a demand made that they lay down their weapons. Thankfully, they did so, and the police linked arms and were able to force the protestors further away. The crowd was compliant and a major disturbance was avoided, but many waited outside of the

The main gates of Strangeways Gaol, outside of which the people of Oldham made their opposition to Kelly's execution clear.

prison gates all night. A vigil was also kept outside of the home of Kelly's distraught mother throughout the night, and 100 onlookers gathered in the street outside the family home.

By 7 a.m., several thousand more people had assembled outside Strangeways and a number of rushes were made at the gates, but again the police managed to prevent significant trouble being caused. At a few minutes past eight, the prison bell rang, indicating that John Ellis the executioner had completed his task. This had the effect of placating the crowd, which gradually began to disperse.

Inside the prison, Kelly had approached the scaffold with a firm step and died bravely. His last letter had been written on the eve of his hanging, and was addressed to his brother. In it he asked him to let the people of his home town know that he was aware of their support and he thanked them for it. Following the execution, a letter from the Home Office official who met the town's delegation was sent to the mayor of Oldham explaining why the Home Secretary had reached different decisions in the cases of the two young men, and he wrote:

> Sir – I have laid before the Secretary of State the papers relating to the case of Edward Hilton and Ernest Kelly which you left with me this afternoon, and have fully stated to him all that you said to me, and he has given the most careful consideration to your representations and fully appreciates the feeling of the people of Oldham about this case.
>
> He desires me to say in reply, that the murder committed by these two men was a very atrocious one, that both of them admitted they took an active part in the murder, and that so far as regards the merits of the case, both would have been left to undergo the full penalty imposed by the law.
>
> But in Hilton's case the Secretary of State had before him clear evidence that from his childhood Hilton was mentally defective and not fully responsible. It was also shown that at the time of the murder he was under eighteen, and it has long been held to be contrary to public policy for any person under the age of eighteen to be executed in England. No such execution has in fact taken place in modern times.
>
> In view of these considerations, which have nothing to do with the actual facts of the murder, the Secretary of State felt it his duty to advise the commutation of Hilton's sentence to penal servitude for life. Neither of these considerations applies in the case of Kelly, who was over twenty years of age at the time of the murder, and fully responsible, and the Secretary of State deeply regrets that having regard to the terrible character of the murder in which he took an active and responsible part, he cannot advise any interference with the course of the law.
> I am Sir, your obedient servant,
> Edward Troup.

There were to be no further demonstrations but the sense of injustice lingered for many years in Oldham, as it was felt that, despite the appalling crime, the different sentences imposed on the perpetrators had meant that a great injustice had occurred.

9

'LITTLE ANNIE IS MISSING', DARWEN, 1932

Six-year-old Naomi Annie Farnworth, known to everyone as Annie, was a popular and friendly little girl, who lived with her parents at 86 Kay Street, in the East Lancashire mill town of Darwen. Spirited and fun-loving, she performed regularly in concerts at Redearth Road Primitive Methodist Sunday School, of which she was a member.

She was a pupil at Highfield Day School, and on the morning of Tuesday 22 March 1932, she was about to leave home and walk the short distance to begin her lessons. At 8.45 a.m. she went upstairs to say goodbye to her mother, who was busy cleaning, and as she walked out of the front door she shouted, 'Goodbye dad'. These proved to be the last words her parents would hear her say.

She spent the morning at her lessons, and at noon she walked to Vernon Street School, where she ate her lunch, which that day consisted of soup and potato hash. She should have returned to Highfield School by 1.15 p.m., but failed to do so. Her teacher, Florence Colley, was not unduly concerned as she presumed she must have gone home, possibly because she was ill.

However, she had not done so, nor had she arrived home by 6 p.m. Her worried parents made unsuccessful enquiries of their neighbours and Annie's friends. Her mother and father, together with several neighbours, began a search of the surrounding area, but having found no trace of her and now desperately concerned for her safety, her parents contacted the police at 9 p.m. A large-scale search was immediately organised and her description was circulated throughout the area. She had a fair complexion and was wearing steel-framed spectacles. That morning she had left the house wearing a navy blue cap and a coat with brass buttons; a blue frock with a pink collar; fawn stockings; and, in common with many Lancashire children at the time, she was wearing clogs.

The search continued by torchlight throughout that night, and as dawn broke, a large group of Boy Scouts, under the direction of the Revd T.P. Payne, joined in the search. However, there was no sign of the missing girl that day, nor, as it continued, throughout the following day. The police, meanwhile, were making door-to-door enquiries and had managed to trace her movements until the lunchtime of the day she went missing.

Their enquiries led them to the fish and tripe shop of Harold and Ena Bumfritt at 95 Kay Street. Annie was well known to them, and although she rarely visited the shop for her family or herself, she came regularly on behalf of Charles Cowle, who lived at 82 Kay Street, just two

The people of Darwen were shocked by the horrific murder of little Annie Farnworth.

doors down from the Farnworth family. On Tuesday lunchtime at about 12.30 p.m., she had called in and asked for a 3d mixture of chips and peas, which she explained to Mrs Bumfritt was for Charles Cowle. There were no peas so Annie left empty-handed, only to return five minutes later asking for tripe and chips.

The police had also visited Mary Foster, who lived with her son James on Elizabeth Street. James was a friend of Charles Cowle, who had visited their house at 4.25 p.m. on the day of Annie's disappearance. This was later than he had arranged with James, and when Mrs Foster asked why he was late he replied that he had been chopping wood. He remained in Mrs Foster's house until 9 p.m., having spent the whole time playing dominoes with her son.

Doris Sharples, a girl of thirteen who knew Annie well and who also knew Charles Cowle, told the police that late on Tuesday night he had approached her in the street and asked if she had heard of Annie's disappearance. She told him she had heard the news, to which he replied menacingly, 'You will be next'.

As the search for Annie continued throughout the Wednesday, Charles Cowle and James Foster joined in, and that evening they helped in the search of Sunnyhurst Wood. Nevertheless, their enquiries had led the police to decide that he was a young man of great interest to them. At 9.45 on Thursday morning, PCs Longbottom and Phillipson visited him at his home. He was asked for details of his movements two days earlier, and he made the following statement:

> I am eighteen years of age, an unemployed spinner, residing at 82 Kay Street. At about 12.30 on the 22nd of March I sent Annie Farnworth of 86 Kay Street, to the chip shop, opposite to

Sunnyhurst Wood, searched by Cowle although he knew that her body was in his house.

where I live. I sent her for a quarter pound of tripe, and twopenneth of chips, and she came back into the house and stayed for a few minutes. I told her to go to school now, and she left the house. I have never seen her since and I don't know which direction she went.

The police were far from satisfied with his account, and ninety minutes later he was visited again by the police. However, on this occasion the officers were Inspector Kay and Detective Sergeant Kenyon. They advised him of their misgivings, and he therefore expressed a wish to make a second statement:

I saw a boy aged about seven years, I know as Jackie, who lives in Sun Street. He was in Kay Street, and I asked him to tell little Annie I wanted her. Annie came to my home and I gave her a jug and asked her to go to the chip shop across the street in Kay Street and fetch me a threepenny mixture. She came back and said they had no peas, and I then asked her to go for a quarter of tripe and chips. She did so, and when she came back with them I put them on a plate and gave her some chips in a paper. She stayed in the house about twenty minutes and then went out. I left the house about 2 p.m., and went into the next door to our house, 1 Elizabeth Street and stayed there until 4 p.m.

The officers advised him that they did not believe this second account, and that they intended searching the house. It was as they walked into the kitchen that he blurted out, 'She's upstairs'. He led the officers to the front bedroom, in which there were three beds. He explained that he had recently started sleepwalking and his stepmother, concerned for his safety, had suggested he sleep in his parents' room so they could ensure there were no accidents or other mishaps. He pointed to a trunk, which was covered in a printed cloth, saying, 'She's in there. I strangled her'.

The cloth was removed and the trunk, which was his mother's, was opened. Inside were items of Mrs Cowle's clothing and his father's war service certificate. The police officers also discovered Annie's body. There was a piece of cord around her neck, and they noticed that the clothing from the lower part of her body had been removed. The suspect pointed to a suitcase which lay nearby, which when unlocked was discovered to contain Annie's missing items of clothing. Cowle and the items of evidence were taken to Darwen Police Station, where he was charged with the little girl's murder, to which he replied, 'I have nothing to say'.

The prime suspect was an immature and feckless youth. His first job had been at Place's Colliery, but he was sacked for idleness. His next job was as a warehouseman at New Mill, where he was considered to be a reasonably good worker, but he was sacked for persistent lateness and using foul language. His last period of employment was as a 'little piecer' with the Edgeworth Spinning Company, from which he was dismissed for throwing weights around in a dangerous manner.

The inquest into Annie's death opened before the county coroner, Frank Bowland, within two hours of her body having been discovered. It was limited to evidence of identification, which was provided by her father, Albert Farnworth. The coroner then adjourned the proceedings so that a post mortem could be performed, and the police could continue with their enquiries. The post mortem was performed by Dr W.E. Cooke, pathologist at the Wigan and Leigh Infirmary. He found her lying face upwards in the trunk, and noted that her hands were tightly clenched. The cord around her neck was wrapped tightly five times. Blood trickled from her mouth, but finding no traces of blood on her clothing, he concluded that strangulation had been the cause of death.

The internal examination revealed a quantity of potato and meat in her stomach, consistent with the hash she had eaten for her school lunch. There were also some partially digested chips, and from the contents of her stomach he concluded that she must have died within three hours of eating for the last time. He revealed that her hymen had been ruptured, which with other injuries to her body confirmed that she had been raped prior to death.

The post mortem having been completed, Annie's body was returned to her parents for burial, and local undertaker Harry Harwood gave his services free of charge. As one might have expected, her funeral was an emotional affair. Her body was placed in a small oak coffin, which made the journey from Kay Street to St Paul's church in Hoddlesden, along streets lined with thousands of people.

At the graveside, Revd H. Townsend, who had been asked by Annie's parents to express their thanks to the many people who had helped in the search for their daughter, and for the support they had received following the discovery of her body, said it demonstrated to the family, 'That the heart of humanity was still sound in Darwen'. Naturally, children played a prominent part in the proceedings, especially her school friends. Hundreds of wreaths were sent and these included one from the Cowle family, the card on which read simply, 'With Deepest Sympathy'. Also among the many tributes was the following poem, penned by a local resident:

> O Little one! Thy tragic fate
> Calls forth even a stranger's tears,
> Yea, the whole town mourneth for thee
> Remembering thy tender years.
> No more can harm befall thee child

THE CHILD'S DEATH.

CASE PRESENTED TO THE MAGISTRATES.

ACCUSED COMMITTED TO THE MANCHESTER ASSIZES.

DEFENCE RESERVED.

Cowle's committal for trial is reported in the local press.

Thou art beyond its reach fore'er,
Beloved beyond all earthly love,
In the Heavenly Father's care.
Thou art just one more sweet flower,
Growing in heaven's garden fair,
And when thy loved ones come again
They will find thee smiling there.

Cowle came to trial at the Manchester Spring Assizes on Tuesday 26 April before trial judge Mr Justice Humphreys. Maxwell Fyfe prosecuted on behalf of the Crown and Mr T.M. Backhouse defended the accused.

Mr Fyfe outlined the strong prosecution case, describing the movements of the deceased and accused on the day of her disappearance. He emphasised the significance of the chips found in her stomach, which she had not eaten at school, and which Cowle had admitted giving her. This must have been very close to the time of her death. There was also, of course, the discovery of the body in his house and the confession he had made when arrested. Most unusually, the prosecution would rely on an interview between the accused and his defence lawyers, to which Inspector Kay had been invited. This appears to have been an attempt by the defence to persuade the Crown that their client was insane.

In his evidence, Inspector Kay testified that, in this interview with his legal representative, Cowle stated that after giving Annie the chips, he had the irresistible urge to carry her upstairs, where he raped her. She began to scream and he put his hands around her throat after which she became quiet. He thought she was dead and placed her in the trunk, and went downstairs to wash his hands. It was then that he realised the seriousness of what he had done and he told his lawyer, 'I thought I had better try and make myself happy and try and forget it'.

The defence had of course realised very early on that there was little option other than to acknowledge that their client had raped and killed Annie, and no attempt was made to suggest otherwise. Rather, they attempted to persuade the jury that he was insane at the time the murder occurred. He had been examined by the police surgeon, Dr J. Willett, at the time of his arrest, who assessed his mental health as normal. This assessment was supported by Dr A. McDonald, deputy medical officer at Strangeways Gaol, who had kept Cowle under constant observation during the whole of the time he had been held there on remand. He found him to be normal and rational, and concluded that he was not mentally defective.

Nevertheless, the defence provided the court with details of members of the family of their client, and his own medical history. The prisoner's father Charles William Cowle confirmed that his son had suffered no serious accidents or illnesses, but he had always been rather dull. When he was a child, the prisoner had attacked a two-year-old boy, hitting him on the head, and had left him for dead in a local stream. The boy survived and Cowle was sent to a Reformatory School, where he was detained for five years.

He also had a history of cruelty to animals, which it is now recognised can, in some cases, be an indicator of severe emotional difficulties in the future, and he had once put a cat down a street grate. When he was eight years old, he was bitten by an Airedale. However, he was not satisfied simply to have the bite wound treated, for he sought the dog out and beat it savagely with a stick. At about the same time, he was found in a cattle pen at the railway station, in which he was beating the cattle with a heavy stick, and from out of which he had to be dragged by station staff.

There was also a history of mental illness within his family. A grandfather and a grandmother spent periods in an asylum in 1912 and 1913. His natural mother was described as 'turning funny in the head' shortly before she died. To support these claims, the defence called Dr A.C. Sturrock, a physician at Salford Royal and Manchester Northern Hospitals, where he was a specialist in nervous and mental disorders. Although he considered the accused fit to plead, he described Cowle as a mental defective with a double personality, who was prone to periods of dullness and periods of violence and excitement. He found him to be dull, apathetic, detached from his surroundings, and to have the mental age of a ten-year-old.

As evidence of his diagnosis, Dr Sturrock highlighted what he considered to be several significant physical features, such as Cowle's head and forehead being smaller than normal. Also, his palate was highly arched, which the doctor described as a definite indicator of moral degeneracy. Dr Willett, the police surgeon, was criticised for not examining the accused's palate, at which point the judge was heard to exclaim, 'Are all people with high-arched palates mentally degenerate? It seems ridiculous'

Undeterred by this interruption, Dr Sturrock continued with his evidence, saying that he had also examined Cowle's hands. He told the court of the accused's habit of biting his finger nails, and described his fingers as being short and square-tipped, such as would be expected to be found in a degenerate type. As for the crime itself, the doctor considered it to be the result of an outburst of insane violence. He believed that from the moment the impulse to assault Annie seized the accused, he would have appreciated nothing until the event was over. He told the court that Cowle was suffering from a condition known as Simplex Dementia Precox. Dr Willett was recalled to comment on Dr Sturrock's evidence and he was scornful of the whole of his professional colleague's testimony.

In his summing up the judge advised the jury that there could be no doubt that Cowle had raped and killed Annie, and as there could have been no provocation, manslaughter was not available as a verdict. The defence had argued that the killing had occurred in a frenzy of sadistic lust and had stemmed from an uncontrollable impulse to rape and murder her. The prosecution case, on the other hand, was that the murder was committed by a sane man, albeit one with a dreadful and horribly vicious mind.

The jury had to decide whether Cowle was insane at the time, and in reaching such a conclusion they must be satisfied that he had not known what he was doing, or that he was incapable of recognising that his actions were wrong. He reminded them that they were entitled to view him as an abnormal individual, and that he may well have been in his youth; however, this did not mean that he was insane. After a brief deliberation the jury returned with a verdict of guilty of wilful murder, and he was sentenced to death.

DARWEN MURDER CHARGE.

YESTERDAY'S ASSIZE COURT HEARING.

COWLE TO DIE.

JURY ABSENT ONLY FIFTEEN MINUTES.

THE JUDGE AND THE QUESTION OF MENTALITY.

News of Cowle's conviction and sentence came as no surprise.

Strangeways Gaol, where Cowle was executed.

That Cowle had committed a most heinous crime was beyond doubt. However, when one so young was sentenced to death, there was usually a great deal of support for a reprieve, and this case was no different. Despite the horrific nature of his crime, there was a good deal of sympathy for him, even from within Darwen. A petition was organised and anyone who wished to sign it was invited to do so by attending the office of his solicitor, Mr Lindsey, and many did so.

However, there was to be no reprieve, and Cowle was hanged at Strangeways Gaol on Wednesday 18 May 1932. A small crowd comprised largely of opponents to capital punishment gathered outside of the gates. Among these was Roy Calvert, secretary of the National Council for the Abolition of the Death Penalty. He was one of many who voiced misgivings about the finding that Cowle had been sane, and he told a reporter:

> This execution is an outrage against humanity. The Home Office has recently defended hanging for boys of eighteen on the grounds that motor bandits in their teens can be as wicked as those who are older.
>
> But Cowle was no motor bandit. He was a mental defective with the mental age of a child, and highly qualified medical evidence has been given that he was possessed of uncontrollable impulses. His was a horrible but meaningless crime.
>
> He was executed because our courts still judge insanity by an 1843 definition, because few prison doctors are trained in mental diseases, and because the Home Secretary inexplicably neglected to refer the case to a board of medical referees.

BIBLIOGRAPHY

Bent, Superintendent James, *Criminal Life; Reminiscences of Forty-Two Years as a Police Officer*
Caminada, Jerome, *Twenty-Five Years of Detective Life, Vols I & II*
Bulfield, R, (Shorthand writer), *The Trial of Alexander and Michael McKeand*

The Ashton-Under-Lyne Reporter
Bells Weekly Messenger
The Bolton Evening Guardian
The Darwen News
Darwen Weekly Advertiser
The Illustrated Police News
The Liverpool Daily Post
The Liverpool Echo
Manchester Evening News
The Manchester Guardian
The Manchester Gazette
The Manchester Herald
The Salford Chronicle
The Salford Weekly News
The Southport Guardian
The Southport Standard
The Standard (Oldham)

Other local titles published by Tempus

Murder & Crime in Nottingham
ADAM NIGHTINGALE

This fascinating collection of tales is illustrated with more than 60 photographs and drawings from the *Illustrated Police News*. Recounting events in the life of the magnetic master criminal, Charlie Peace, as well as a plethora of other horrifying true-life cases, this chilling catalogue of crimes is sure to horrify and captivate anyone interested in the criminal history of the area.

978 07524 4496 3

Murder & Crime in Pendle and the Ribble Valley
JACQUELINE DAVITT

This fascinating book contains tales of thwarted rivals and wicked soldiers, desperate mothers and disreputable women. With more than 50 illustrations, this chilling catalogue of murderous misdeeds is bound to captivate anyone interested in the criminal history of the area.

978 07524 4495 6

Ghosts & Gravestones of York
PHILIP LISTER

Take a terrifying tour of the deserted streets and darkest ginnels in Europe's most haunted city. With intriguing tales of the Minster's haunted pew, a tragic massacre at the Bedern Orphanage and the unfortunate events leading to Dick Turpin's demise, this book is sure to captivate anyone with an interest in the darker side of York's long and fascinating history.

978 07524 4357 7

Lancaster and the Lune Valley
DR D.J. ALSTON

This fascinating collection of more than 180 old photographs traces some of the many ways in which Lancaster has changed over the last century. A valuable historical record of life in the ancient city, this book depicts almost every aspect of daily life and will reawaken nostalgic memories for many.

978 07524 3007 2

If you are interested in purchasing other books published by Tempus, or in case you have difficulty finding any Tempus books in your local bookshop, you can also place orders directly through our website

www.tempus-publishing.com